How to Succeed in the Christian Life

Reuben Archer Torrey

Originally published in 1906

Dedicated to the many thousands in many lands who have professed Christ in our meetings.

TABLE OF CONTENTS

I. BEGINNING RIGHT
II. THE OPEN CONFESSION OF CHRIST
III. ASSURANCE OF SALVATION
IV. RECEIVING THE HOLY SPIRIT
V. LOOKING UNTO JESUS
VI. CHURCH MEMBERSHIP
VII. BIBLE STUDY
VIII. DIFFICULTIES IN THE BIBLE
IX. PRAYER
X. WORKING FOR CHRIST
XI. FOREIGN MISSIONS
XII. COMPANIONS
XIII. AMUSEMENTS
XIV. PERSECUTION
XV. GUIDANCE

FOOTNOTES

Reuben Archer Torrey

INTRODUCTION

I have for years felt the need of a book to put in the hands of those beginning the Christian life that would tell them just how to make a complete success of this new life upon which they were entering. I could find no such book, so I have been driven to write one. This book aims to tell the young convert just what he most needs to know. I hope that pastors and evangelists and other Christian workers may find it a good book to put in the hands of young converts. I hope that it may also prove a helpful book to many who have long been Christians but have not made that headway in the Christian life that they long for.

Reuben Archer Torrey

I
BEGINNING RIGHT

There is nothing more important in the Christian life than beginning right. If we begin right we can go on right. If we begin wrong the whole life that follows is likely to be wrong. If any one who reads these pages has begun wrong, it is a very simple matter to begin over again and begin right. What the right beginning in the Christian life is we are told in John 1: 12, "But as many as RECEIVED HIM, to them gave He power to become the sons of God, even to them that believe on His name." The right way to begin the Christian life is by receiving Jesus Christ. To any one who receives Him, He at once gives power to become a child of God. If the reader of this book should be the wickedest man on earth and should at this moment receive Jesus Christ, that very instant he would become a child of God. God says so in the most unqualified way in the verse quoted above. No one can become a child of God in any other way. No man, no matter how carefully he has been reared, no matter how well he has been sheltered from the vices and evils of this world, is a child of God until he receives Jesus Christ. We are "sons of God through faith in Christ Jesus" (Gal. 3: 26, R. V.), and in no other way.

What does it mean to receive Jesus Christ? It means to take Christ to be to yourself all that God offers Him to be to everybody. Jesus Christ is God's gift. "For God so loved the world that He gave His only begotten Son that whosoever believeth in Him should not perish but have everlasting life" (John 3: 16). Some accept this wondrous gift of God. Every one who does accept this gift becomes a child of God. Many others refuse this wondrous gift of God, and every one who refuses this gift of God perishes. He is condemned already. "He that believeth on the Son is not condemned, but he that believeth not is condemned already because he hath not believed in the name of the only begotten Son of God" (John 3: 18).

What does God offer His Son to be to us?

1. First of all, *God offers Jesus to us to be our sin-bearer*. We have all sinned. There is not a man or woman or a boy or a girl who has not sinned (Romans 3: 22, 23). If any of us say that we have not sinned we are deceiving ourselves and giving the lie to God (1 John 1: 8, 10). Now we must each of us bear our own sin or some one else must bear it in our place. If we were to bear our own sins, it would mean we must be banished forever from the presence of God, for God is holy. "God is light and in Him is no darkness at all" (1 John 1:5). But God Himself has provided another to bear our sins in our place so that we should not need to bear them ourselves. This sin-bearer is God's own Son, Jesus Christ, "For He hath made Him to be sin for us who knew no sin that we might be made the righteousness of God in Him" (2 Cor. 5:21). When Jesus Christ died upon the cross of Calvary He redeemed us from the curse of the law by being made a curse in our stead (Gal. 3:13). To

receive Christ then is to believe this testimony of God about His Son, to believe that Jesus Christ did bear our sins in His own body on the cross (1 Pet. 2:24), and to trust God to forgive all our sins because Jesus Christ has borne them in our place. "All we like sheep have gone astray; we have turned every one to his own way; and the Lord hath laid on Him the iniquity of us all" (Is. 53:6). Our own good works, past, present or future have nothing to do with the forgiveness of our sins. Our sins are forgiven, not because of any good works that we do, they are forgiven because of the atoning work of Christ upon the cross of Calvary in our place. If we rest in this atoning work we shall do good works, but our good works will be the outcome of our being saved and the outcome of our believing on Christ as our sin-bearer. Our good works will not be the ground of our salvation, but the result of our salvation, and the proof of it. We must be very careful not to mix in our good works at all as the ground of salvation. We are not forgiven because of Christ's death *and our good works*, we are forgiven solely and entirely because of Christ's death. To see this clearly is the right beginning of the true Christian life.

2. *God offers Jesus to us as our deliverer from the power of sin.* Jesus not only died, He rose again. To-day He is a living Saviour. He has all power in heaven and on earth (Matt. 28: 18). He has power to keep the weakest sinner from falling (Jude 24). He is able to save not only from the uttermost but "to the uttermost" all that come unto the Father through Him. (Wherefore He is able to save

to the uttermost them that draw near unto God through Him, seeing that He ever liveth to make intercession for them.—Heb. 7: 25, R. V.) "If the Son therefore shall make you free, ye shall be free indeed" (John 8: 36). To receive Jesus is to believe this that God tells us in His Word about Him, to believe that He did rise from the dead, to believe that He does now live, to believe that He has power to keep us from falling, to believe that He has power to keep us from the power of sin day by day, and just trust Him to do it.

This is the secret of daily victory over sin. If we try to fight sin in our own strength, we are bound to fail. If we just look up to the risen Christ to keep us every day and every hour, He will keep us. Through the crucified Christ we get deliverance from the guilt of sin, our sins are all blotted out, we are free from all condemnation; but it is through the risen Christ that we get daily victory over the power of sin. Some receive Christ as a sin-bearer and thus find pardon, but do not get beyond that, and so their life is one of daily failure. Others receive Him as their risen Saviour also, and thus enter into an experience of victory over sin. To begin right we must take Him not only as our sin-bearer, and thus find pardon; but we must also take Him as our risen Saviour, our Deliverer from the power of sin, our Keeper, and thus find daily victory over sin.

3. But *God offers Jesus to us, not only as our sin-bearer and our Deliverer from the power of sin, but He also offers Him to us as our Lord and King.* We read in Acts 2: 36, "Let all the house of Israel know assuredly, that God hath made that same Jesus, whom

ye have crucified, both Lord and Christ." Lord means Divine Master, and Christ means anointed King. To receive Jesus is to take Him as our Divine Master, as the One to whom we yield the absolute confidence of our intellects, the One whose word we believe absolutely, the One whom we will believe though many of the wisest of men may question or deny the truth of His teachings; and as our King to whom we gladly yield the absolute control of our lives, so that the question from this time on is never going to be, what would I like to do or what do others tell me to do, or what do others do, but the whole question is WHAT WOULD MY KING JESUS HAVE ME DO? A right beginning involves an unconditional surrender to the Lordship and Kingship of Jesus.

The failure to realize that Jesus is Lord and King, as well as Saviour, has led to many a false start in the Christian life. We begin with Him as our Saviour, as our sin-bearer and our Deliverer from the power of sin, but we must not end with Him merely as Saviour, we must know Him as Lord and King. There is nothing more important in a right beginning of the Christian life than an unconditional surrender, both of the thoughts and the conduct to Jesus. Say from your heart and say it again and again, "*All* for Jesus." Many fail because they shrink back from this entire surrender. They wish to serve Jesus with half their heart, and part of themselves and part of their possessions. To hold back anything from Jesus means a wretched life of stumbling and failure.

The life of entire surrender is a joyous life all along the way. If you have never done it before, go alone with God to-day, get down on your knees and say, "All for Jesus," and mean it. Say it very earnestly; say it from the bottom of your heart. Stay there until you realize what it means and what you are doing. It is a wondrous step forward when one really takes it. If you have taken it already, take it again, take it often. It always has fresh meaning and brings fresh blessedness. In this absolute surrender is found the key to the truth. Doubts rapidly disappear for one who surrenders all (John 7: 17). In this absolute surrender is found the secret of power in prayer (1 John 3: 22). In this absolute surrender is found the supreme condition of receiving the Holy Ghost (Acts 5: 32).

Taking Christ as your Lord and King involves obedience to His will as far as you know it in each smallest detail of life. There are those who tell us that they have taken Christ as their Lord and King who at the same time are disobeying Him daily in business, in domestic life, in social life and in personal conduct Such persons are deceiving themselves. You have not taken Jesus as your Lord and King if you are not striving to obey Him in everything each day. He Himself says, "Why call ye Me 'Lord, Lord!' and do not the things that I say?" (Luke 6: 46).

To sum it all up, the right way to begin the Christian life is to accept Jesus Christ as your sin-bearer and to trust God to forgive your sins because Jesus Christ died in your place; to accept Him as your risen Saviour who ever lives to make intercession for you, and who has all power to keep you, and to trust Him to keep you from day to day; and to accept Him as your Lord and King to whom you surrender the absolute control of your thoughts and of your life. This is the right beginning, the only right beginning of the Christian life. If you have made this beginning, all that follows will be comparatively easy. If you have not made this beginning, make it now.

Reuben Archer Torrey

II

THE OPEN CONFESSION OF CHRIST

Having begun the Christian life right by taking the proper attitude towards Christ in a private transaction between Himself and yourself, the next step is an open confession of the relationship that now exists between yourself and Jesus Christ. Jesus says in Matt. 10: 32, "Whosoever therefore shall confess Me before men, him will I confess also before My Father which is in heaven." He demands a public confession. He demands it for your own sake. This is the path of blessing. Many attempt to be disciples of Jesus and not let the world know it. No one has ever succeeded in that attempt. To be a secret disciple means to be no disciple at all. If one really has received Christ he cannot keep it to himself. "For out of the abundance of the heart the mouth speaketh" (Matt. 12: 34). So important is the public confession of Christ that Paul puts it first in his statement of the conditions of salvation. He says, "If thou shalt *confess with thy mouth* the Lord Jesus and shalt believe in thine heart that God hath raised Him from the dead, thou shalt be saved. For with the heart man believeth unto righteousness; and with the mouth confession is made unto salvation" (Rom. 10: 9, 10). The life of confession is the life of full salvation. Indeed, the life of confession is the life of the only real salvation. When we confess Christ before men down here, He confesses us before the Father in heaven and the Father gives us the Holy Spirit as the seal of our salvation.

It is not enough that we confess Christ just once, as, for example, when we are confirmed, or when we unite with the church, or when we come forward in a revival meeting. We should confess Christ constantly. We should not be ashamed of our Lord and King. We should let people know that we are on His side. In the home, in the church, at our work, and at our play, we should let others know where we stand. Of course, we should not parade our Christianity or our piety, but we should leave no one in doubt whether we belong to Christ. We should let it be seen that we glory in Him as our Lord and King.

The failure to confess Christ is one of the most frequent causes of backsliding. Christians get into new relationships where they are not known as Christians and where they are tempted to conceal the fact; they yield to the temptation and they soon find themselves drifting. The more you make of Jesus Christ, the more He will make of you. It will save you from many a temptation if the fact is clearly known that you are one who acknowledges Christ as Lord in all things.

III

ASSURANCE OF SALVATION

If one is to have the fullest measure of joy and power in Christian service, he must know that his sins are forgiven, that he is a child of God, and that he has eternal life. It is the believer's privilege to *know* that he has eternal life. John says in 1 John 5: 13, R. V., "These things have I written unto you, *that ye may know* that ye have eternal life, even unto you that believe on the name of the Son of God." John wrote this first epistle for the express purpose that any one who believes on the name of the Son of God *might know* that he has eternal life.

There are those who tell us that no one can know that he has eternal life until he is dead and has been before the judgment seat of God, but God Himself tells us that we may know. To deny the possibility of the believer's knowing that he has eternal life is to say that the First Epistle of John was written in vain, and it is to insult the Holy Spirit who is its real author. Again Paul tells us in Acts 13: 39, R. V., "By Him (that is by Christ) every one that believeth *is justified* from all things." So every one that believeth in Jesus may know that he is justified from all things. He may know it because the Word of God says so. Again John tells us in John 1: 12, R. V., "But *as many as received Him* (that is Jesus Christ) to them gave He the right to become children of God, even to them that believe on His name." Here is a definite and unmistakable declaration that every one who receives Jesus becomes a child of God. Therefore every believer in Jesus may know that he is a child of God. He may know it on the surest of all grounds, *i. e.*, because the Word of God asserts that he is a child of God.

But how may any individual know that he has eternal life? He may know it on the very best ground of knowledge, that is through the testimony of God Himself as given in the Bible. The testimony of Scripture is the testimony of God. What the Scriptures say is absolutely sure. What the Scriptures say God says. Now in John 3: 36 the Scriptures say, "He that believeth on the Son *hath* everlasting life." Any one of us may know whether we believe on the Son or not. Whether we have that real faith in Christ that leads us to receive Him. If we have this faith in Christ we have God's own written testimony that we have eternal life, that our sins are forgiven, that we are the children of God. We may feel forgiven, or we may not feel forgiven, but that does not matter. It is not a question of what we feel but of what God says. God's Word is always to be believed. Our own feelings are oftentimes to be doubted. There are many who are led to doubt their sins are forgiven, to doubt that they have everlasting life, to doubt that they are saved, because they do not feel forgiven, or do not feel that they have everlasting life, or do not feel that they are saved. Because you do not feel it is no reason why you should doubt it.

Suppose that you were sentenced to imprisonment and that your friends secured a pardon for you. The legal document announcing your pardon is brought to you. You read it and know you are pardoned because the legal document says so, but the news is so good and so sudden that you are dazed by it. You do not realize that you are pardoned. Some one comes to you and says, "Are you pardoned?" What would you reply? You would say, "Yes, I am pardoned." Then he asks, "Do you feel pardoned?" You reply, "No, I do not feel pardoned. It is so sudden, it is so wonderful, I cannot realize it." Then he says to you, "But how can you know that you are pardoned if you do not feel it?" You would hold out the document and you would say, "This says so." The time would come, after you had read the document over and over again and believed it, when you would not only know you were pardoned because the document said so but you would feel it. Now the Bible is God's authoritative document declaring that every one that believeth in Jesus is justified; declaring that every one that believeth on the Son hath everlasting life; declaring that every one who receives Jesus is a child of God. If any one asks you if your sins are all forgiven, reply, "Yes, I know they are because God says so." If they ask you if you know that you are a child of God, reply, "Yes, I know I am a child of God because God says so." If they ask you if you have everlasting life, reply, "Yes, I know I have everlasting life because God says so. God says, 'He that believeth on the Son hath everlasting life.' I know I believe on the

Son, and therefore I know I have eternal life—because God says so." You may not feel it yet but if you will keep meditating upon God's statement and believing what God says, the time will come when you will feel it.

For one who believes on the Son of God to doubt that he has eternal life is for him to make God a liar. "He that believeth on the Son of God hath the witness in him. He that believeth not God, hath made Him a liar because he hath not believed in the witness that God hath borne concerning His Son and the witness is this, that God gave unto us eternal life, and this life is in His Son. He that hath the Son hath the life: he that hath not the Son of God hath not the life" (1 John 5: 10-12, R. V.). Any one who does not believe God's testimony that He has given unto us eternal life and that this life is in His Son and that he that hath the Son hath the life, makes God a liar.

It is sometimes said "it is presumption for any one to say that he knows he is saved, or to say that he knows that he has eternal life." But is it presumption to believe God? Is it not rather presumption not to believe God, to make God a liar? When you who believe on the Son of God and yet doubt that you have eternal life, you make God a liar. When Jesus said to the woman who was a sinner, "Thy sins are forgiven" (Luke 7: 48), was it presumption for her to go out and say, "I know my sins are all forgiven"? Would it not have been presumption for her to have doubted for a moment that her sins were all forgiven? Jesus had said that they were forgiven. For her to doubt it would have been for her to give the lie to Jesus. Is it then any more presumption for the believer to-day to say, "My sins are all forgiven, I have eternal life," when God says in His written testimony to every one that believeth, "You are justified from all things" (Acts 13: 39), "You have eternal life" (John 3: 36; 1 John 5: 13)?

Be very sure first of all that you really do believe on the name of the Son of God; that you really have received Jesus. If you are sure of this then never doubt for a moment that your sins are all forgiven, never doubt for a moment that you are a child of God, never doubt for a moment that you have everlasting life. If Satan comes and whispers, "Your sins are not forgiven," point Satan to the Word of God and say, "God says my sins are forgiven and I know they are." If Satan whispers, "Well perhaps you don't believe on Him," then say, "Well if I never did before I will now." And then go out rejoicing, knowing that your sins are forgiven, knowing that you are a child of God, knowing that you have everlasting life.

There are doubtless many who say they know they have eternal life who really do not believe on the name of the Son of God, who have not really received Jesus. This is not true assurance. It has no sure foundation in the Word of God who cannot lie. If we wish to get assurance of salvation we must first get saved. The reason why many have not the assurance that they are saved is because they are not saved. They ought not to have assurance. What they need first is salvation. But if you have received Jesus in the way described in the first chapter, YOU ARE SAVED, you are a child of God, your sins are forgiven. Believe it, know it. Rejoice in it.

Having settled it, let it remain settled. Never doubt it. You may make mistakes, you may stumble, you may fall, but even if you do, if you have really received Jesus, know that your sins are forgiven and rise from your fall and go forward in the glad assurance that there is nothing between you and God.

IV

RECEIVING THE HOLY SPIRIT

When the Apostle Paul came to Ephesus, he found a little group of twelve disciples of Christ. There was something about these twelve disciples that struck Paul unfavourably. We are not told what it was. It may be that he did not find in them that overflowing joyfulness that one learns to expect in all Christians who have really entered into the fullness of blessing that there is for them in Christ. It may be that Paul was troubled at the fact that there were only twelve of them, thinking that if these twelve were what they ought to be, there would certainly have been more than twelve of them by this time. Whatever it may have been that impressed Paul unfavourably, he went right to the root of the difficulty at once by putting to them the question, "Did ye receive the Holy Ghost when ye believed?" (Acts 19: 2, R. V.). It came out at once that they had not received the Holy Ghost, that in fact they did not know that the Holy Ghost had been given. Then Paul told them that the Holy Ghost had been given, and also showed them just what they must do to receive the Holy Ghost then and there, and before that gathering was over the Holy Ghost came upon them. From that day on there was a different state of affairs in Ephesus. A great revival sprang up at once so that the whole city was shaken, "So mightily grew the Word of God and prevailed" (Acts 19: 20). Paul's question to these young disciples in Ephesus should be put to young disciples everywhere, "Have ye received the Holy Ghost?"

In *receiving the Holy Spirit* is the great secret of joyfulness in our own hearts, of victory over sin, of power in prayer, and of effective service.

Every one who has truly received Jesus must have the Holy Spirit dwelling in him in some sense; but in many believers, though the Holy Spirit dwells in them, He dwells way back in some hidden sanctuary of their being, back of consciousness. It is something quite different, something far better than this, to receive the Holy Spirit in the sense that Paul meant in his question. To receive the Holy Spirit in such a sense that one knows experimentally that he has received the Holy Spirit, to receive the Holy Spirit in such a sense that we are conscious of the joy with which He fills our hearts different from any joy that we have ever known in the world; to receive the Holy Spirit in such a sense that He rules our life and produces within us in ever increasing measure the fruit of the Spirit, love, joy, peace, long-suffering, gentleness, goodness, faith, meekness, temperance; to receive the Holy Spirit in such a sense that we are conscious of His drawing our hearts out in prayer in a way that is not of ourselves; to receive the Holy Spirit in such a sense that we are conscious of His help when we witness for Christ, when we speak to others individually and try to lead them to accept Christ, or when we teach a Sunday-school class, or speak in public, or do any other work for the Master. Have you received the Holy Spirit? If you have not, let me tell you how you may.

1. First of all in order to receive the Holy Spirit, one must be resting in the death of Christ on the cross for us as the sole and all-sufficient ground upon which God pardons all our sins and forgives us.

2. In order to receive the Holy Spirit we must put away every known sin. We should go to our heavenly Father and ask Him to search us through and through and bring to light anything in our life, our outward life or our inward life, that is wrong in His sight, and if He does bring anything to light that is displeasing to Him, we should put it away, no matter how dear it is to us. There must be a complete renunciation of all sin in order to receive the Holy Spirit.

3. In the third place, in order to receive the Holy Spirit, there must be an open confession of Christ before the world. The Holy Spirit is not given to those who are trying to be disciples in secret, but to those who obey Christ and publicly confess Him before the world.

4. In the fourth place, in order to receive the Holy Spirit, there must be an absolute surrender of our lives to God. You must go to Him and say, "Heavenly Father, here I am. Thou hast bought me with a price. I am Thy property. I renounce all claim to do my own will, all claim to govern my own life, all claim to have my own way. I give myself up unreservedly to Thee—all I am and all I have. Send me where Thou wilt, use me as Thou wilt, do with me

what Thou wilt—I am Thine." If we hold anything back from God, no matter how small it may seem, that spoils it all. But if we surrender all to God, then God will give all that He has to us. There are some who shrink from this absolute surrender to God, but absolute surrender to God is simply absolute surrender to infinite love. Surrender to the Father, to the Father whose love is not only wiser than any earthly father's, but more tender than any earthly mother's.

5. In order to receive the Holy Spirit there should be definite asking for the Holy Spirit. Our Lord Jesus says in Luke 11: 13, "If ye then, being evil, know how to give good gifts unto your children: how much more shall your heavenly Father give the Holy Spirit to them that ask Him?" Just ask God to give you the Holy Spirit and expect Him to do it, because He says He will.

6. Last of all, in order to receive the Holy Spirit, there must be faith, simply taking God at His Word. No matter how positive any promise of God's Word may be, we enjoy it personally only when we believe. Our Lord Jesus says, "All things whatsoever ye pray and ask for, believe that ye have received them, and ye shall have them" (Mark 11: 24, R. V.). When you pray for the Holy Spirit you have prayed for something according to God's will and therefore you may know that your prayer is heard and that you have what you asked of Him (1 John 5: 14, 15). You may feel no different, but do not look at your feelings but at God's promise. Believe the prayer is heard, believe that God has given you the Holy Spirit and

you will afterwards have in actual experience what you have received in simple faith on the bare promise of God's Word.

It is well to go often alone and kneel down and look up to the Holy Spirit and put into His hands anew the entire control of your life. Ask Him to take the control of your thoughts, the control of your imagination, the control of your affections, the control of your desires, the control of your ambitions, the control of your choices, the control of your purposes, the control of your words, the control of your actions, the control of everything, and just expect Him to do it. The whole secret of victory in the Christian life is letting the Holy Spirit who dwells within you, have undisputed right of way in the entire conduct of your life.

Reuben Archer Torrey

V
LOOKING UNTO JESUS

If we are to run with patience the race that is set before us, we must always keep looking unto Jesus (Heb. 12: 1-3). One of the simplest and yet one of the mightiest secrets of abiding joy and victory is to *never lose sight of Jesus*.

1. First of all *we must keep looking at Jesus as the ground of our acceptance before God*. Over and over again Satan will make an attempt to discourage us by bringing up our sins and failures and thus try to convince us that we are not children of God, or not saved. If he succeeds in getting us to keep looking at and brooding over our sins, he will soon get us discouraged, and discouragement means failure. But if we will keep looking at what God looks at, the death of Jesus Christ in our place that completely atones for every sin that we ever committed, we will never be discouraged because of the greatness of our sins. We shall see that while our sins are great, very great, that they have all been atoned for. Every time Satan brings up one of our sins, we shall see that Jesus Christ has redeemed us from its curse by being made a curse in our place (Gal. 3: 13). We shall see that while in ourselves we are full of unrighteousness, nevertheless in Christ we are made the righteousness of God, because Christ was made to be sin in our place (2 Cor. 5: 21). We will see that every sin that Satan taunts us

about has been borne and settled forever (1 Pet. 2: 24; Is. 53: 6). We shall always be able to sing,

> "Jesus paid my debt,
>
> ALL THE DEBT I OWE;
>
> Sin had left a crimson stain,
>
> HE WASHED IT WHITE AS SNOW."

If you are this moment troubled about any sin that you have ever committed, either in the past or in the present, just look at Jesus on the cross; believe what God tells you about Him, that this sin which troubles you was laid upon Him (Is. 53: 6). Thank God that the sin is all settled; be full of gratitude to Jesus who bore it in your place and trouble about it no more. It is an act of base ingratitude to God to brood over sins that He in His infinite love has cancelled. Keep looking at Christ on the cross and walk always in the sunlight of God's favour. This favour of God has been purchased for you at great cost. Gratitude demands that you should always believe in it and walk in the light of it.

2. In the second place, *we must keep looking at Jesus as our risen Saviour, who has all power in heaven and on earth and is able to keep us every day and every hour.* Are you tempted to do some wrong at this moment? If you are, remember that Jesus rose

from the dead, remember that at this moment He is living at the right hand of God in the glory; remember that He has all power in heaven and on earth, and that, therefore, He can give you victory right now. Believe what God tells you in His Word that Jesus has power to save you this moment "to the uttermost" (Heb. 7: 25). Believe that He has power to give you victory over this sin that now besets you. Ask Him to give you victory, expect Him to do it. In this way by looking unto the risen Christ for victory you may have victory over sin every day, every hour, every moment. "Remember Jesus Christ risen from the dead" (2 Tim. 2: 8, R. V.).

God has called every one of us to a victorious life, and the secret of this victorious life is always looking to the risen Christ for victory. Through looking to Christ crucified we obtain pardon and enjoy peace. Through looking to the risen Christ we obtain present victory over the power of sin. If you have lost sight of the risen Christ and have yielded to temptation, confess your sin and know that it is forgiven because God says so (1 John 1: 9) and look to Jesus, the risen One, again to give you victory now and keep looking to Him.

3. In the third place, *we must keep looking to Jesus as the One whom we should follow in our daily conduct.* Our Lord Jesus says to us, His disciples to-day, as He said to His early disciples, "Follow Me." The whole secret of true Christian conduct can be summed up in these two words "Follow Me." "He that saith he abideth in Him ought himself so to walk *even as He walked*" (1

John 2: 6). One of the commonest causes of failure in Christian life is found in the attempt to follow some good man, whom we greatly admire. No man and no woman, no matter how good, can be safely followed. If we follow any man or woman, we are bound to go astray. There never has been but one absolutely perfect Man upon this earth—the Man Christ Jesus. If we try to follow any other man we are more sure to imitate his faults than his excellencies. Look at Jesus and Jesus only as your Guide.

If at any time you are in any perplexity as to what to do, simply ask the question, What would Jesus do? Ask God by His Holy Spirit to show you what Jesus would do. Study your Bible to find out what Jesus did do and follow Jesus. Even though no one else seems to be following Jesus, be sure that you follow Him. Do not spend your time or thought in criticising others because they do not follow Jesus. See that you follow Him yourself. When you are wasting your time criticising others for not following Jesus, Jesus is always saying to you, "What is that to thee; follow THOU Me" (John 21; 22). The question for you is not what following Jesus may involve for other people. The question is what does following Jesus mean for you?

This is the really simple life, the life of simply following Jesus. Many perplexing questions will come to you, but the most perplexing question will soon become as clear as day if you determine with all your heart to follow Jesus in everything. Satan will always be ready to whisper to you, "Such and such a good man does it," but all you need to do is to answer, "It matters not to me what this or that man may do or not do. The only question to me is, What would Jesus do?" There is wonderful freedom in this life of simply following Jesus. This path is straight and plain. But the path of the one who tries to shape his conduct by observing the conduct of others is full of twists and turns and pitfalls. Keep looking at Jesus. Follow on trustingly where He leads. This is the path of the just which shineth more and more unto the perfect day (Prov. 4: 18). He is the Light of the World, any one who follows Him shall not walk in darkness, but shall have the light of life all along the way (John 8: 12).

Reuben Archer Torrey

VI

CHURCH MEMBERSHIP

No young Christian and no old Christian can have real success in the Christian life without the fellowship of other believers. The church is a divine institution, built by Jesus Christ Himself. It is the one institution that abides. Other institutions come and go; they do their work for their day and disappear, but the church will continue to the end. "The gates of hell shall not prevail against it" (Matt. 16: 18). The church is made up of men and women, imperfect men and women, and consequently is an imperfect institution, but none the less it is of divine origin and God loves it, and every believer should realize that he belongs to it and should openly take his place in it and bear his responsibilities regarding it.

The true church consists of all true believers, all who are united to Jesus Christ by a living faith in Himself. In its outward organization at the present time, it is divided into numberless sects and local congregations, but in spite of these divisions the true church is one. It has one Lord, Jesus Christ. It has one faith, faith in Him as Saviour, Divine Lord and only King; one baptism, the baptism in the one Spirit into the one body (Eph. 4: 4, 5; 1 Cor. 12: 13). But each individual Christian needs the fellowship of individual fellow believers. The outward expression of this fellowship is in membership in some organized body of believers. If we hold aloof from all organized churches, hoping thus to have a broader fellowship with all believers belonging to all the churches, we deceive ourselves. We will miss the helpfulness that comes from intimate union with some local congregation. I have known many well-meaning persons who have held aloof from membership in any specific organization, and I have never known a person who has done this, whose own spiritual life has not suffered by it. On the day of Pentecost the three thousand who were converted were at once baptized and were added to the church (Acts 2: 41, 47), and "They continued steadfastly in the apostle's doctrine and fellowship, and in breaking of bread and in prayers." Their example is the one to follow. If you have really received Jesus Christ, hunt up as soon as possible some company of others who have received Jesus Christ and unite yourself with them.

In many communities there may be no choice of churches, for there is only one. In other communities one will be faced with the question, "With what body of believers shall I unite?" Do not waste your time looking for a perfect church. There is no perfect church. If you wait until you find a perfect church before you unite with any, you will unite with none, and thus you will belong to a church in which you are the only member and that is the most imperfect church of all. I would rather belong to the most imperfect Christian church I ever knew than not to belong to any church at all. The local churches in Paul's day were very imperfect institutions. Let one read the epistles to the Corinthians and see how imperfect was the church in Corinth, see how much there was that was evil in it, and yet Paul never thought of advising any believer in Corinth to get out of this imperfect church. He did tell them to come out of heathenism, to come out from fellowship with infidels (2 Cor. 6: 14-18), but not a word on coming out of the imperfect church in Corinth. He did tell the church in Corinth to separate from their membership certain persons whose lives were wrong (1 Cor. 5: 11, 12), but he did not tell the individual members of the church in Corinth to get out of the church because these persons had not yet been separated from their fellowship.

As you cannot find a perfect church, find the best church you can. Unite with a church where they believe in the Bible and where they preach the Bible. Avoid the churches where words are spoken open or veiled that have a tendency to undermine your faith in the Bible as a reliable revelation from God Himself, the all-sufficient rule of faith and practice. Unite with a church where there is a spirit of prayer, where the prayer-meetings are well kept up. Unite with a church that has a real active interest in the salvation of the lost, where young Christians are looked after and helped, where minister and people have a love for the poor and outcast, a church that regards its mission in this world to be the same as the mission of Christ, "to seek and to save the lost." As to denominational differences, other things being equal, unite with that denomination whose ideas of doctrine and of government and of the ordinances are most closely akin to your own. But it is better to unite with a live church of some other denomination than to unite with a dead church of your own. We live in a day when denominational differences are becoming ever less and less, and oftentimes they are of no practical consequence whatever; and one will often feel more at home in a church of some other denomination than in any accessible church of his own denomination. The things that divide the denominations are insignificant compared with the great fundamental truths and purposes and faith that unite them.

If you cannot find the church that agrees with the pattern set forth above, find the church that comes nearest to it. Go into that church and by prayer and by work try to bring that church as nearly as you can to the pattern of what you think a church of Christ ought to be. But do not waste your strength in criticism against either church or minister. Seek for what is good in the church and in the minister and do your best to strengthen it. Hold aloof firmly, though unobtrusively, from what is wrong and seek to correct it. Do not be discouraged if you cannot correct it in a day or a week or a month or a year. Patient love and prayer and effort will tell in time. Drawing off by yourself and snarling and grumbling will do no good. They will simply make you and the truths for which you stand repulsive.

Reuben Archer Torrey

VII

BIBLE STUDY

There is nothing more important for the development of the spiritual life of the Christian than regular, systematic Bible study. It is as true in the spiritual life as it is in the physical life that health depends upon what we eat and how much we eat. The soul's proper food is found in one book, the Bible. Of course, a true minister of the gospel will feed us on the Word of God, but that is not enough. He feeds us but one or two days in the week and we need to be fed every day. Furthermore, it will not do to depend upon being fed by others. We must learn to feed ourselves. If we study the Bible for ourselves as we ought to study it, we shall be in a large measure independent of human teachers. Even if we are so unfortunate as to have for our minister a man who is himself ignorant of the truth of God we shall still be safe from harm.

We live in a day in which false doctrine abounds on every hand and the only Christian who is safe from being led into error is the one who studies his Bible for himself daily. The Apostle Paul warned the elders of the church in Ephesus that the time was soon coming when grievous wolves should enter in among them not sparing the flock and when of their own selves men should arise speaking perverse things to draw away the disciples after them, but he told them how to be safe even in such perilous times as these. He said, "I commend you to God and to the Word of His grace, which is able to build you up and to give you an inheritance among them which are sanctified." Through meditation on the Word of God's grace they would be safe even in the midst of abounding error on the part of the leaders in the church (Acts 20: 29-32). Writing later to the Bishop of the church in Ephesus Paul said, "But evil men and impostors shall wax worse and worse, deceiving and being deceived" (2 Tim. 3: 13, R. V.) but he goes on to tell Bishop Timothy how he and his fellow believers could be safe even in such times of increasing peril as were coming. That way was through the study of the Holy Scriptures, which are able to make wise unto salvation (2 Tim. 3: 14, 15). "All Scripture," he adds, "is given by inspiration of God and is profitable for doctrine, for reproof, for correction, for instruction in righteousness that the man of God may be perfect, thoroughly furnished unto all good works." That is to say, through the study of the Bible one will be sound in doctrine, will be led to see his sins and put them away, will find discipline in the righteous life and attain unto complete equipment for all good works. Our spiritual health, our growth, our strength, our victory over sin, our soundness in doctrine, our joy and peace in Christ, our cleansing from inward and outward sin, our fitness for service, all depend upon the study of the Word of God. The one who neglects his Bible is bound to make a failure of the Christian life. The one who studies his Bible in the right spirit and by a true method is bound to make a success of the Christian life.

This brings us face to face with the question, "What is the right way to study the Bible?"

1. First of all, we should *study it daily* (Acts 17: 11). This is of prime importance. No matter how good the methods of Bible study that one follows may be, no matter how much time one may put into Bible study now and then, the best results can only be secured when one makes it a matter of principle never to let a single day go by without earnest Bible study. This is the only safe course. Any day that is allowed to pass without faithful Bible study is a day thrown open to the advent into our hearts and lives of error or of sin. The writer has been a Christian for more than a quarter of a century and yet to-day he would not dare to allow even a single day to pass over his head without listening to the voice of God as it speaks to him through the pages of His Book. It is at this point that many fall away. They grow careless and let a day pass, or even several days pass, without going alone with God and letting Him speak to them through His Word. Mr. Moody once wisely said, "In prayer we talk to God. In Bible study, God talks to us, and we had better let God do most of the talking."

A regular time should be set apart each day for the study of the Bible. I do not think it is well as a rule to say that we shall study so many chapters in a day, for that leads to undue haste and skimming and thoughtlessness, but it is well to set apart a certain length of time each day for Bible study. Some can give more time to Bible study than others, but no one ought to give less than fifteen minutes a day. I set the time so low in order that no one may be discouraged at the outset. If a young Christian should set out to give an hour or two hours a day to Bible study, there is a strong probability that he would not keep to the resolution and he might become discouraged. Yet I know of many very busy people who have given the first hour of every day for years to Bible study and some who have given even two hours a day. The late Earl Cairns, Lord Chancellor of England, was one of the busiest men of his day, but Lady Cairns told me a few months ago that no matter how late he reached home at night he always arose at the same early hour for prayer and Bible study. She said, "We would sometimes get home from Parliament at two o'clock in the morning, but Lord Cairns would always arise at the same early hour to pray and study the Bible." Lord Cairns is reported as saying, "If I have had any success in life, I attribute it to the habit of giving the first two hours of each day to Bible study and prayer."

It is important that one choose the right time for this study. Wherever it is possible, the best time for this study is immediately after arising in the morning. The worst time of all is the last thing at night. Of course, it is well to give a little while just before we retire to Bible reading, in order that God's voice may be the last to which we listen, but the bulk of our Bible study should be done at an hour when our minds are clearest and strongest. Whatever time is set apart for Bible study should be kept sacredly for that purpose.

2. We should *study the Bible systematically*. Much time is frittered away in random study of the Bible. The same amount of time put into systematic study would yield far larger results. Have a definite place where you are studying and have a definite plan of study. A good way for a young Christian to begin the study of the Bible is to read the Gospel of John. When you have read it through once, begin and read it again until you have gone over the Gospel five times. Then read the Gospel of Luke five times in the same way; then read the Acts of the Apostles five times, then 1 Thessalonians five times, then 1 John five times, then Romans five times, then Ephesians five times.

By this time you will be ready to take up a more thorough method of Bible study. A good method is to begin at Genesis and read the Bible through chapter by chapter. Read each chapter through several times and then answer the following questions on the chapter:

(1) What is the principal subject of the chapter? (State the principal contents of the chapter in a single phrase or sentence.)

(2) What is the truth most clearly taught and most emphasized in the chapter?

(3) What is the best lesson?

(4) What is the best verse?

(5) Who are the principal people mentioned?

(6) What does the chapter teach about Jesus Christ? Go through the entire Bible in this way.

Another and more thorough method of Bible chapter study, which cannot be applied to every chapter in the Bible, but which will yield excellent results when applied to some of the more important chapters of the Bible, is as follows:

(1) Read the chapter for to-day's study five times, reading it aloud at least once. Each new reading will bring out some new point.

(2) Divide the chapter into its natural divisions and find headings for each division that describes in the most striking way the contents of that division. For example, suppose the chapter studied is 1 John 5. You might divide it in this way: First division, verses 1-3, The Believer's Noble Parentage. Second division, verses 4, 5, The Believer's Glorious Victory. Third division, verses 6-10, The Believer's Sure Ground of Faith. Fourth division, verses 11, 12, The Believer's Priceless Possession. Fifth division, verse 13, The Believer's Blessed Assurance. Sixth division, verses 14, 15, The Believer's Unquestioning Confidence. Seventh division, verses 16, 17, The Believer's Great Power and Responsibility. Eighth division, verses 18, 19, The Believer's Perfect Security. Ninth division, verse 20, The Believer's Precious Knowledge. Tenth division, verse 21, The Believer's Constant Duty.

(3) Note the important differences between the Authorized Version and the Revised.

(4) Write down the leading facts of the chapter in their proper order.

(5) Make a note of the persons mentioned in the chapter and of any light thrown upon their character.

(6) Note the principal lessons of the chapter. It would be well to classify these. For instance lessons about God; lessons about Christ, lessons about the Holy Spirit, etc.

(7) Find the central truth of the chapter.

(8) The key verse of the chapter, if there is one.

(9) The best verse in the chapter. Mark it and memorize it.

(10) Write down what new truth you have learned from the chapter.

(11) Write down what truth already known has come to you with new power.

(12) What definite thing have you resolved to do as a result of studying this chapter. It would be well to study in this way, all the chapters in Matthew, Mark, Luke, John and Acts; the first eight chapters of Romans; 1 Cor. 12, 13 and 15; first six chapters of 2 Corinthians; all the chapters in Galatians, Ephesians, Philippians,

First Thessalonians and First Epistle of John. It would be well at times to vary this by taking up other methods of study for a time.

Another profitable method of Bible study is the topical method. This was Mr. Moody's favourite method of study. Take up the great topics of which the Bible teaches such as, the Holy Spirit, Prayer, the Blood of Christ, Sin, Judgment, Grace, Justification, the New Birth, Sanctification, Faith, Repentance, the Character of Christ, the Resurrection of Christ, the Ascension of Christ, the Second Coming of Christ, Assurance, Love of God, Love (to God, to Christ, to Christians, to all men), Heaven, Hell. Get a Bible text-book and go through the Bible on each one of these topics. (Other methods of Bible study, and more thorough methods for the advanced student, will be found in the author's book "HOW TO STUDY THE BIBLE FOR GREATEST PROFIT.")

3. We should *study the Bible comprehensively*—the whole Bible. Many who read their Bibles make the great mistake of confining all their reading to certain portions of the Bible that they enjoy, and in this way they get no knowledge of the Bible as a whole. They miss altogether many of the most important phases of Bible truth. Begin and go through the Bible again and again—a certain portion each day from the Old Testament and a portion from the New Testament. Read carefully at least one Psalm every day.

It is well oftentimes to read a whole book of the Bible through at a single sitting. Of course, with a few books of the Bible this would take one or two hours, but with most of the books of the Bible it can be done in a few minutes. With the shorter books of the Bible they should be read through again and again at a single sitting.

4. *Study the Bible attentively.* Do not hurry. One of the worst faults in Bible study is haste and heedlessness. The Bible only does good by the truth that it contains. It has no magic power. It is better to read one verse attentively than to read a dozen chapters thoughtlessly. Sometimes you will read a verse that takes hold of you. Don't hurry on. Linger and ponder that verse. As you read, mark in your Bible what impresses you most. One does not need an elaborate system of Bible marking, simply mark what impresses you. Meditate upon what you mark. God pronounces that man blessed who "meditates" in God's law day and night (Ps. 1: 2). It is wonderful how a verse of Scripture will open if one reads it over and over again and again, paying attention to each word as he reads it, trying to get its exact meaning and its full meaning. Memorize the passages that impress you most (Ps. 119: 11, R. V.). When you memorize a passage of Scripture, memorize its location as well as its words. Fix in your mind chapter and verse where the words are found. A busy but spiritually-minded man who was hurrying to catch a train once said to me, "Tell me in a word how to study my Bible." I replied, "Thoughtfully."

5. *Study your Bible comparatively.* That is compare Scripture with Scripture. The best commentary on the Bible is the Bible itself. Wherever you find a difficult passage in the Bible, there is always some passage elsewhere that explains its meaning. The best book to use in this comparison of Scripture with Scripture is "The Treasury of Scripture Knowledge." On every verse in the Bible this book gives a large number of references. It is well to take up some book of the Bible and go through that book verse by verse, looking up carefully and studying every reference given in "The Treasury of Scripture Knowledge." This is a very fruitful method of Bible study. It is also well in studying the Bible by chapters to look up the references on the more important verses in the chapter. One will get more light on passages of Scripture by looking up the references given in "The Treasury of Scripture Knowledge," than in any other way I know.

6. *Study your Bible believingly.* The Apostle Paul in writing to the Christians in Thessalonica says, "For this cause also thank we God without ceasing, because, when ye received the Word of God which ye heard of us, ye received it not as the Word of men, but as it is in truth, the Word of God, which effectually worketh also in you that believe" (1 Thess. 2: 13). Happy is the one who receives the Word of God as these believers in Thessalonica received it, who receives it as what it really is, the Word of God. In such a one it "works effectually." The Bible is the Word of God and we get the most out of any book by studying it as what it really is. It is

often said that we should study the Bible just as we study any other book. That principle contains a truth, but it also contains a great error. The Bible, it is true, is a book as other books are books, the same laws of grammatical and literary construction hold here as in other books, but the Bible is a unique book. It is what no other book is, the Word of God. This can be easily proven to any candid man.[1] The Bible ought then to be studied as no other book is. It should be studied as the Word of God. This involves five things:

(1) A greater eagerness and more careful and candid study to find out just what it teaches than is bestowed upon all other books. It is important to know the mind of man. It is absolutely essential to know the mind of God. The place to discover the mind of God is the Bible. This is the book in which God reveals His mind.

(2) A prompt and unquestioning acceptance of, and submission to its teachings when definitely ascertained. These teachings may appear to us unreasonable or impossible, nevertheless we should accept them. If this book is the Word of God, how foolish it is to submit its teachings to the criticism of our finite reasoning. A little boy who discredits his wise father's statements simply because to his infant mind they appear unreasonable, is not a philosopher, but a fool. But the greatest of human thinkers is only an infant compared with the infinite God. And to discredit God's statements found in His Word because they appear unreasonable to our infantile minds is not to act the part of the philosopher, but the part of a fool. When we are once satisfied that the Bible is the Word of

God, its clear teachings must be for us the end of all controversy and discussion.

(3) Absolute reliance upon all its promises in all their length and breadth and depth and height. The one who studies the Bible as the Word of God will say of any promise, no matter how vast and beyond belief it appears, "God who cannot lie has promised this, so I will claim it for myself." Mark the promise you thus claim. Look each day for some new promise from your infinite Father. He has put "His riches in glory" at your disposal (Phil. 4: 19). I know of no better way to grow rich spiritually than to search daily for promises, and when you find them appropriate them to yourself.

(4) Obedience. Be a doer of the Word and not a hearer only deceiving your own soul (James 1: 22). Nothing goes farther to help one understand the Bible than the purpose to obey it. Jesus said, "If any man willeth to do His will, he shall know of the teaching" (John 7: 17 R. V.). The surrendered will means the clear eye. If our eye is single (that is, our will is absolutely surrendered to God) our whole body shall be full of light. But if our eye be evil (that is, if we are trying to serve two masters and are not absolutely surrendered to one Master, God) our whole body shall be full of darkness (Matt. 6: 22-24). Many a passage that looks obscure to you now would become as clear as day if you were willing to obey in all things what the Bible teaches. Each commandment discovered in the Bible that is really intended as a commandment to us should be obeyed instantly. It is remarkable how soon one

loses his relish for the Bible and how soon the mind becomes obscured to its teachings when we disobey the Bible at any point. Many a time I have known persons who have loved their Bibles and have been useful in God's service and clear in their views of the truth who have come to something in the Bible that they were unwilling to obey, some sacrifice was demanded that they were unwilling to make, and their love for the Bible has rapidly waned, their faith in the Bible began to weaken, and soon they were drifting farther and farther away from clear views of the truth. Nothing clears the mind like obedience; nothing darkens the mind like disobedience. To obey a truth you see prepares you to see other truths. To disobey a truth you see darkens your mind to all truths.

Cultivate prompt, exact, unquestioning, joyous obedience to every command that it is evident from its context applies to you. Be on the lookout for new orders from your King. Blessing lies in the direction of obedience to them. God's commands are but signboards that mark the road to present success and blessedness and to eternal glory.

(5) Studying the Bible as the Word of God involves studying it as His own voice speaking directly to you. When you open the Bible to study realize that you have come into the very presence of God and that now He is going to speak to you. Realize that it is God who is talking to you as much as if you saw Him standing there. Say to yourself, "God is now going to speak to me." Nothing

goes farther to give a freshness and gladness to Bible study than the realization that as you read God is actually talking to you. In this way Bible study becomes personal companionship with God Himself. That was a wonderful privilege that Mary had one day, of sitting at the feet of Jesus and listening to His voice, but if we will study the Bible as the Word of God and as if we were in God's very presence, then we shall enjoy the privilege of sitting at the feet of God and having Him talk to us every day. How often what would otherwise be a mere mechanical performance of a duty would become a wonderfully joyous privilege if one would say as he opens the Bible, "Now God, my Father, is going to speak to me." Oftentimes it helps us to a realization of the presence of God to read the Bible on our knees. The Bible became in some measure a new book to me when I took to reading it on my knees.

7. *Study the Bible prayerfully.* God, who is the author of the Bible, is willing to act as interpreter of it. He does so when you ask Him to. The one who prays with earnestness and faith the Psalmist's prayer, "Open Thou mine eyes that I may behold wondrous things out of Thy law" (Ps. 119: 18) will get his eyes opened to see new beauties and wonders in the Word of God that he never dreamed of before. Be very definite about this. Each time you open the Bible to study it, even though it is but for a few minutes, ask God to give you an open and discerning eye, and expect Him to do it. Every time you come to a difficulty in the Bible, lay it before God and ask an explanation and expect it. How

often we think as we puzzle over hard passages, "Oh, if I only had some great Bible teacher here to explain this to me!" God is always present. He understands the Bible better than any human teacher. Take your difficulty to Him and ask Him to explain it. Jesus said, "When He the Spirit of Truth is come, He shall guide you into all the truth" (John 16: 13, R. V.). It is the privilege of the humblest believer in Christ to have the Holy Spirit for his guide in his study of the Word. I have known many very humble people, people with almost no education, who got more out of their Bible study than most of the great theological teachers that I have known; simply because they had learned that it was their privilege to have the Holy Spirit for their teacher as they studied the Bible. Commentaries on the Bible are oftentimes of great value, but one will learn more of real value from the Bible by having the Holy Spirit for his teacher when he studies his Bible than he will from all the commentaries that were ever published.

8. *Improve spare moments for Bible study.* In almost every man's life many minutes each day are lost, while waiting for meals, riding on trains, going from place to place in street-cars and so forth. Carry a pocket Bible or Testament with you and save these golden moments by putting them to the very best use, listening to the voice of God.

9. *Store away the Scripture in your mind and heart.* It will keep you from sin (Ps. 119: 11, R. V.); from false doctrine (Acts 20: 29, 30, 32; 2 Tim. 3: 13-15). It will fill your heart with joy (Jer. 15:

16); and peace (Ps. 85: 8). It will give you victory over the evil one (1 John 2: 14); it will give you power in prayer (John 15: 7); it will make you wiser than the aged and your enemies (Ps. 119: 98, 100, 130); it will make you "complete, furnished completely unto every good work" (2 Tim. 3: 16, 17, R. V.). Try it. Do not memorize at random but memorize Scripture in a connected way; memorize texts bearing on various subjects in proper order; memorize by chapter and verse that you may know where to put your finger on the text if any one disputes it. You should have a good Bible for your study. One of the best is "The Oxford Two Version Bible, Workers' Edition."

VIII

DIFFICULTIES IN THE BIBLE

Sooner or later every young Christian comes across passages in the Bible which are hard to understand and difficult to believe. To many a young Christian, these difficulties become a serious hindrance in the development of their Christian life. For days and weeks and months oftentimes faith suffers partial or total eclipse. At just this point wise counsel is needed. We have no desire to conceal the fact that these difficulties exist. We rather desire to frankly face and consider them. What shall we do concerning these difficulties that every thoughtful student of the Bible will sooner or later encounter.

1. *The first thing we have to say about these difficulties is that from the very nature of the case difficulties are to be expected.* Some people are surprised and staggered because there are difficulties in the Bible. I would be more surprised and more staggered if there were not. What is the Bible? It is a revelation of the mind and will and character and being of the infinitely great, perfectly wise, and absolutely holy God. But to whom is this revelation made? To men and women like you and me, to finite beings. To men who are imperfect in intellectual development and consequently in knowledge, and in character and consequently in spiritual discernment.

There must, from the very necessities of the case, be difficulties in such a revelation made to such persons. When the finite tries to understand the infinite there is bound to be difficulty. When the ignorant contemplate the utterances of one perfect in knowledge there must be many things hard to be understood and some things which to their immature and inaccurate minds appear absurd. When sinful beings listen to the demands of an absolutely holy being they are bound to be staggered at some of His demands, and when they consider His dealings they are bound to be staggered at some of His dealings. These dealings will necessarily appear too severe, stern, harsh, terrific. It is plain that there must be difficulties for us in such a revelation as the Bible is proven to be. If some one should hand me a book that was as simple as the multiplication table and say, "This is the Word of God, in which He has revealed His whole will and wisdom," I would shake my head and say, "I cannot believe it. That is too easy to be a perfect revelation of infinite wisdom." There must be in any complete revelation of God's mind and will and character and being, things hard for a beginner to understand, and the wisest and best of us are but beginners.

2. *The second thing to be said about these difficulties is that a difficulty in a doctrine, or a grave objection to a doctrine, does not in any wise prove the doctrine to be untrue.* Many thoughtless people fancy that it does. If they come across some difficulty in the way of believing in the divine origin and absolute inerrancy and

infallibility of the Bible, they at once conclude that the doctrine is exploded. That is very illogical. Stop a moment and think and learn to be reasonable and fair. There is scarcely a doctrine in science commonly believed to-day that has not had some great difficulty in the way of its acceptance. When the Copernican theory, now so universally accepted, was first proclaimed, it encountered a very grave difficulty. If this theory were true the planet Venus should have phases as the moon has. But no phases could be discovered by the best glass then in existence. But the positive argument for the theory was so strong that it was accepted in spite of this apparently unanswerable objection. When a more powerful glass was made, it was discovered that Venus had phases after all. The whole difficulty arose, as all those in the Bible arise, from man's ignorance of some of the facts in the case. According to the common sense logic recognized in every department of science, if the positive proof of a theory is conclusive, it is believed by rational men, in spite of any number of difficulties in minor details. Now the positive proof that the Bible is the Word of God, that it is an absolutely trustworthy revelation from God Himself of Himself, His purposes and His will, of man's duty and destiny, of spiritual and eternal realities, is absolutely conclusive. Therefore every rational man and woman must believe it in spite of any number of difficulties in minor details. He is a shallow thinker who gives up a well-attested truth because of some facts which he cannot reconcile with that truth. And he is a very shallow

Bible scholar who gives up the divine origin and inerrancy of the Bible because there are some supposed facts that he cannot reconcile with that doctrine.

3. *The third thing to be said about the difficulties in the Bible is that there are many more and much greater difficulties in the way of a doctrine that holds the Bible to be of human origin, and hence fallible, than are in the way of the doctrine that holds the Bible to be of divine origin and hence altogether trustworthy.* A man may bring you some difficulty and say, "How do you explain that if the Bible is the Word of God?" and perhaps you may not be able to answer him satisfactorily. Then he thinks he has you, but not at all. Turn on him and ask him how do you account for the fulfilled prophecies of the Bible if it is of human origin? How do you account for the marvellous unity of the Book? How do you account for its inexhaustible depth? How do you account for its unique power in lifting men up to God? How do you account for the history of the Book, its victory over all men's attacks, etc., etc., etc. For every insignificant objection he can bring to your view, you can bring many deeply significant objections to his view, and no candid man will have any difficulty in deciding between the two views. The difficulties that confront one who denies that the Bible is of divine origin and authority are far more numerous and weighty than those that confront the ones who believes it is of divine origin and authority.

4. *The fourth thing to be said about the difficulties in the Bible is the fact that you cannot solve a difficulty does not prove that it cannot be solved, and the fact that you cannot answer an objection does not prove at all that it cannot be answered.* It is passing strange how often we overlook this very evident fact. There are many who, when they meet a difficulty in the Bible and give it a little thought and can see no possible solution, at once jump at the conclusion that a solution is impossible by any one, and so throw up their faith in the reliability of the Bible and in its divine origin. A little more of that modesty that is becoming in beings so limited in knowledge as we all are would have led them to say, "Though I see no possible solution to this difficulty, some one a little wiser than I might easily find one." Oh! if we would only bear in mind that we do not know everything, and that there are a great many things that we cannot solve now that we could easily solve if we only knew a little more. Above all, we ought never to forget that there may be a very easy solution to infinite wisdom of that which to our finite wisdom—or ignorance—appears absolutely insoluble. What would we think of a beginner in algebra who, having tried in vain for half an hour to solve a difficult problem, declared that there was no possible solution to the problem because he could find none? A man of much experience and ability once left his work and came a long distance to see me in great perturbation of spirit because he had discovered what seemed to him a flat contradiction in the Bible. It had defied all his attempts at

reconciliation, but in a few moments he was shown a very simple and satisfactory solution of the difficulty.

5. *The fifth thing to be said about the difficulties in the Bible is that the seeming defects in the book are exceedingly insignificant when put in comparison with its many and marvellous excellencies.* It certainly reveals great perversity of both mind and heart that men spend so much time expatiating on the insignificant points that they consider defects in the Bible, and pass by absolutely unnoticed the incomparable beauties and wonders that adorn and glorify almost every page. What would we think of any man, who in studying some great masterpiece of art, concentrated his entire attention upon what looked to him like a fly-speck in the corner. A large proportion of what is vaunted as "critical study of the Bible" is a laborious and scholarly investigation of supposed fly-specks and an entire neglect of the countless glories of the book.

6. *The sixth thing to be said about the difficulties in the Bible is that the difficulties in the Bible have far more weight with superficial readers of it than with profound students.* Take a man who is totally ignorant of the real contents and meaning of the Bible and devotes his whole strength to discovering apparent inconsistencies in it, to such superficial students of the Bible these difficulties seem of immense importance; but to the one who has learned to meditate on the Word of God day and night they have scarce any weight at all. That mighty man of God, George Müller,

who had carefully studied the Bible from beginning to end more than a hundred times, was not disturbed by any difficulties he encountered. But to the one who is reading it through carefully for the first or second time there are many things that perplex and stagger.

7. The seventh thing to be said about the difficulties in the Bible is that they rapidly disappear upon careful and prayerful study. How many things there are in the Bible that once puzzled us and staggered us that have been perfectly cleared up, and no longer present any difficulty at all! Is it not reasonable to suppose that the difficulties that still remain will also disappear upon further study?

How shall we deal with the difficulties which we do find in the Bible?

1. First of all, *honestly*. Whenever you find a difficulty in the Bible, frankly acknowledge it. If you cannot give a good honest explanation, do not attempt as yet to give any at all.

2. *Humbly*. Recognize the limitations of your own mind and knowledge, and do not imagine there is no solution just because you have found none. There is in all probability a very simple solution. You will find it some day, though at present you can find no solution at all.

3. *Determinedly*. Make up your mind that you will find the solution if you can by any amount of study and hard thinking. The

difficulties in the Bible are your heavenly Father's challenge to you to set your brains to work.

4. *Fearlessly.* Do not be frightened when you find a difficulty, no matter how unanswerable it appears upon first glance. Thousands have found such before you. They were seen hundreds of years ago and still the Old Book stands. You are not likely to discover any difficulty that was not discovered and probably settled long before you were born, though you do not know just where to lay your hand upon the solution. The Bible which has stood eighteen centuries of rigid examination and incessant and awful assault, is not going under before any discoveries that you make or any attacks of modern infidels. All modern infidel attacks upon the Bible are simply a revamping of old objections that have been disposed of a hundred times in the past. These old objections will prove no more effective in their new clothes than they did in the cast-off garments of the past.

5. *Patiently.* Do not be discouraged because you do not solve every problem in a day. If some difficulty defies your best effort, lay it aside for awhile. Very likely when you come back to it, it will have disappeared and you will wonder how you were ever perplexed by it. The writer often has to smile to-day when he thinks how sorely he was perplexed in the past over questions which are now as clear as day.

6. *Scripturally.* If you find a difficulty in one part of the Bible, look for other Scripture to throw light upon it and dissolve it. Nothing explains Scripture like Scripture. Never let apparently obscure passages of Scripture darken the light that comes from clear passages, rather let the light that comes from the clear passage illuminate the darkness that seems to surround the obscure passage.

7. *Prayerfully.* It is wonderful how difficulties dissolve when one looks at them on his knees. One great reason why some modern scholars have learned to be destructive critics is because they have forgotten how to pray.

Reuben Archer Torrey

IX

PRAYER

The one who would succeed in the Christian life must lead a life of prayer. Very much of the failure in Christian living to-day, and in Christian work, results from neglect of prayer. Very few Christians spend as much time in prayer as they ought. The Apostle James told believers in his day that the secret of the poverty and powerlessness of their lives and service was neglect of prayer. "Ye have not," says God through the Apostle James, "because ye ask not." So it is to-day. Why is it, many a Christian is asking, that I make such poor headway in my Christian life? Why do I have so little victory over sin? Why do I accomplish so little by my effort? and God answers, "You have not because you ask not."

It is easy enough to lead a life of prayer if one only sets about it. Set apart some time each day for prayer. The rule of David and of Daniel is a good one; three times a day. "Evening and morning and at noon, says David, will I pray and cry aloud and He shall hear my voice" (Ps. 55: 17). Of Daniel we read, "Now when Daniel knew that the writing was signed, he went into his house; and his windows being open in his chamber towards Jerusalem, he kneeled upon his knees three times a day, and prayed, and gave thanks before his God as he did aforetime" (Dan. 6: 10). Of course, one can pray while walking the street, or riding in the car, or sitting at his desk, and one should learn to lift his heart to God right in the busiest moments of his life, but we need set times of prayer, times when we go alone with God, shut to the door and talk to our Father in the secret place (Matt. 6: 6). God is in the secret place and will meet with us there and listen to our petitions.

Prayer is a wonderful privilege. It is an audience with the King. It is talking to our Father. How strange it is that people should ask the question, "How much time ought I to spend in prayer?" When a subject is summoned to an audience with his king, he never asks, "How much time must I spend with the king?" His question is rather, "How much time will the king give me?" And with any true child of God who realizes what prayer really is, that it is an audience with the King of Kings, the question will never be, "How much time must I spend in prayer," but "How much time may I spend in prayer with a due regard to other duties and privileges?"

Begin the day with thanksgiving and prayer. Thanksgiving for the definite mercies of the past, prayer for the definite needs of the present day. Think of the temptations that you are likely to meet during the day; ask God to show you the temptations that you are likely to meet and get from God strength for victory over these temptations before the temptations come. The reason why many fail in the battle is because they wait until the hour of battle. The reason why others succeed is because they have gained their victory on their knees long before the battle came. Jesus conquered in the awful battles of Pilate's judgment hall and of the cross because He had the night before in prayer anticipated the battle and gained the victory before the struggle really came. He had told His disciples to do the same. He had bidden them "Pray that ye enter not into temptation" (Luke 22: 40), but they had slept when they ought to have prayed, and when the hour of temptation came they fell. Anticipate your battles, fight them on your knees before temptation comes and you will always have victory. At the very outset of the day, get counsel and strength from God Himself for the duties of the day.

Never let the rush of business crowd out prayer. The more work that any day has to do, the more time must be spent in prayer in preparation for that work. You will not lose time by it, you will save time by it. Prayer is the greatest time saver known to man. The more the work crowds you the more time take for prayer.

Stop in the midst of the bustle and hurry and temptation of the day for thanksgiving and prayer. A few minutes spent alone with God at midday will go far to keep you calm in the midst of the worries and anxieties of modern life.

Close the day with thanksgiving and prayer. Review all the blessings of the day and thank God in detail for them. Nothing goes farther to increase faith in God and in His Word than a calm review at the close of each day of what God has done for you that day. Nothing goes further towards bringing new and larger blessings from God than intelligent thanksgiving for blessings already granted.

The last thing you do each day ask God to show you if there has been anything in the day that has been displeasing in His sight. Then wait quietly before God and give God an opportunity to speak to you. Listen. Do not be in a hurry. If God shows you anything in the day that has been displeasing in His sight, confess it fully and frankly as to a holy and loving Father. Believe that God forgives it all, for He says He does (1 John 1: 9). Thus at the close of each day all your accounts with God will be straightened out. You can lie down and sleep in the glad consciousness that there is not a cloud between you and God. You can arise the next day to begin life anew with a clean balance sheet. Do this and you can never backslide for more than twenty-four hours. Indeed, you will not backslide at all. It is very hard to straighten out accounts in business that have been allowed to get crooked through a prolonged period. No bank ever closes its business day until its balance is found to be absolutely correct. And no Christian should close a single day until his accounts with God for that day have been perfectly adjusted alone with Him.

There should be special prayer in special temptation—that is when we see the temptation approaching. If you possibly can, get at once alone somewhere with God and fight your battle out. Keep looking to God. "Pray without ceasing" (1 Thess. 5: 17). It is not needful to be on your knees all the time but the heart should be on its knees all the time. We should be often on our knees or on our faces literally. This is a joyous life, free from worry and care. "In nothing be anxious; but in everything by prayer and supplication with thanksgiving, let your request be made known unto God, and the peace of God which passeth all understanding shall guard your hearts and thoughts in Christ Jesus" (Phil. 4: 6, 7, R. V.).

There are three things for which one who would succeed in the Christian life must especially pray. 1. For wisdom. "If any of you lack wisdom (and we all do) let him ask of God" (James 1: 5). 2. For strength. "For they that wait upon the Lord shall renew their strength" (Is. 40: 31). 3. For the Holy Spirit. "Your heavenly Father shall give the Holy Spirit to them that ask Him" (Luke 11: 13). Even if you have received the Holy Spirit, you should constantly pray for a new filling with the Holy Spirit and definitely expect to receive it. We need a new filling with the Spirit for every new emergency of Christian life and Christian service. The Apostle Peter was baptized and filled with the Holy Spirit on the Day of Pentecost (Acts 2: 1-4) but he was filled anew in Acts 4: 8 and Acts 4: 31. There are many Christians in the world who once had a very definite baptism with the Holy Spirit and had great joy and were wonderfully used, but who have tried to go ever since in the power of that baptism received years ago, and to-day their lives are comparatively joyless and powerless. We need constantly to get new supplies of oil for our lamps. We get these new supplies of oil by asking for them.

It is not enough that we have our times of secret prayer to God alone with Him, we also need fellowship with others in prayer. If they have a prayer-meeting in your church attend it regularly. Attend it for your own sake; attend it for the sake of the church. If it is a prayer-meeting only in name and not in fact, use your influence quietly and constantly (not obtrusively) to make it a real prayer-meeting. Keep the prayer-meeting night sacredly for that purpose. Refuse all social engagements for that night. A major-general in the United States army once took command of the forces in a new district. A reception was arranged for him for a certain night in the week. When he was informed of this public reception he replied that that was prayer-meeting night and everything else had to give way for prayer-meeting, that he could not attend the reception on that night. That general had proved himself a man that can be depended upon. The Church of Christ in America owes more to him than to almost any other officer in the American army. Ministers learn to depend upon their prayer-meeting members. The prayer-meeting is the most important meeting in the church. If your church has no prayer-meeting, use your influence to have one. It does not take many members to make a good prayer-meeting. You can start with two but work for many.

It is well to have a little company of Christian friends with whom you are in real sympathy and with whom you meet regularly every week simply for prayer. There has been nothing of more importance in the development of my own spiritual life of recent years than a little prayer-meeting of less than a dozen friends who have met every Saturday night for years. We met and together we waited upon God. If my life has been of any use to the Master, I attribute it largely to that prayer-meeting. Happy is the young Christian that has a little band of friends like that that meet together regularly for prayer.[2]

Reuben Archer Torrey

X
WORKING FOR CHRIST

One of the important conditions of growth and strength in the Christian life is work. No man can keep up his physical strength without exercise and no man can keep up his spiritual strength without spiritual exercise, *i. e.*, without working for his Master. The working Christian is the happy Christian. The working Christian is the strong Christian. Some Christians never backslide because they are too busy about their Master's business to backslide. Many professed Christians do backslide because they are too idle to do anything but backslide. Jesus said to the first disciples, "Follow Me and I will make you fishers of men" (Matt. 4: 19). Any one who is not a fisher of men is not following Christ. Bearing fruit in bringing others to the Saviour is the purpose for which Jesus has chosen us and is one of the most important conditions of power in prayer. Jesus says in John 15: 16, "Ye have not chosen Me, but I have chosen you and ordained you *that ye should go and bring forth fruit, and that your fruit should remain that whatsoever ye shall ask of the Father in My name He may give it you.*" These words of Jesus are very plain. They tell us that the one who is bearing fruit is the one who can pray in the name of Christ and get what he asks in that name. In the same chapter Jesus tells us that bearing fruit in His strength is the condition of fullness of joy. He says, "These things have I spoken unto you (that is, the things about abiding in Him and bearing fruit in His strength) that

My joy might remain in you and that your joy might be full" (John 15: 11). Experience abundantly proves the truth of these words of our Master. Those who are full of activity in winning others to Christ are those who are full of joy in Christ Himself.

If you wish to be a happy Christian; if you wish to be a strong Christian, if you wish to be a Christian who is mighty in prayer, begin at once to work for the Master and never let a day pass without doing some definite work for Him. But how can a young Christian work for Him? How can a young Christian bear fruit? The answer is very simple and very easy to follow. You can bear fruit for your Master by going to others and telling them what your Saviour has done for you, and by urging them to accept this same Saviour and showing them how to do it. There is no other work in the world that is so easy to do, so joyous, and so abundant in its fruitfulness, as personal hand to hand work. The youngest Christian can do personal work. Of course, he cannot do it so well as he will do it later, after he has had more practice. But the way to learn how to do it is by doing it. I have known thousands of Christians all around the world who have begun to work for Christ, and to bring others to Christ, the very day that they were converted. How often young men and young women, yes, and old men and old women too, have come to me and said, "I accepted Jesus Christ last night as my Saviour, my Lord and my King, and to-night I have led a friend to Christ." Then the next day they would come and tell me of some one else they had led to Christ.

When we were in Sheffield, a young man working in a warehouse accepted Christ. Before the month's mission in Sheffield was over he had led thirty others to Christ, many of them in the same warehouse where he himself worked. This is but one instance among many. There are many books that tell how to do personal work.[3]

But one does not need to wait until they have read some book on the subject before they begin. One of the commonest and greatest mistakes that is made is that of frittering one's life away in getting ready to get ready to get ready. Some never do get ready. The way to get ready is to begin at once. Make up your mind that you will speak about accepting Christ to at least one person every day. Early in his Christian life Mr. Moody made this resolution that he would never let a day pass over his head without speaking to at least one person about Christ. One night he was returning late from his work. As he got near home it occurred to him that he had not spoken to any one that day. He said to himself, "It is too late now. I will not get an opportunity. Here will be one day gone without my speaking to any one about Christ." But a little ways ahead of him he saw a man standing under a lamp-post. He said, "Here is my last opportunity." The man was a stranger to him, though he knew who Mr. Moody was. Mr. Moody hurried up to him and asked him, "Are you a Christian?" The man replied, "That is none of your business. If you were not a sort of a preacher I would knock you into the gutter." But Mr. Moody spoke a few faithful words to him and passed on. The next day this man called on one of Mr. Moody's business friends in Chicago in great indignation. He said, "That man Moody of yours over on the Northside is doing more harm than he is good. He has zeal without knowledge. He came up to me last night, a perfect stranger, and asked me if I was a Christian. He insulted me. I told him if he had not been a sort of preacher I would have knocked him into the gutter." Mr. Moody's friend called him in and said to him, "Moody, you are doing more harm than good. You have zeal without knowledge. You insulted a friend of mine on the street last night." Mr. Moody went out somewhat crestfallen, feeling that perhaps he was doing more harm than good, that perhaps he did have zeal without knowledge. But some weeks after, late at night, there was a great pounding on his door. Mr. Moody got out of bed and rushed to the door supposing that the house was on fire. That same man stood at the door. He said, "Mr. Moody, I have not had a night's rest since you spoke to me that night under the lamp-post and I have come around for you to tell me what to do to be saved." Mr. Moody had the joy that night of leading that man to Christ. It is better to have zeal without knowledge than to have knowledge without zeal, but it is better yet to have zeal with knowledge, and any one may have this. The way to get knowledge is by experience, and the way to get experience is by doing the work. The man who is so afraid of making blunders that he never does anything, never learns anything. The man who goes ahead and does his best and is willing to risk the blunders, is the man who learns to avoid the blunders in the future. Some of the most gifted men I have ever known have never really accomplished anything, they were so fearful of making blunders. Some of the most useful men I have ever known were men who at the outset were the least promising, but who had a real love for souls and went on, at first in a blundering way, but they blundered on until they learned by experience to do things well. Do not be discouraged by your blunders. Pitch in and keep pegging away. Every honest mistake is but a stepping-stone to future success. Try every day to lead some one else to Christ. Of course, you will not succeed every day, but the work will do you good any way, and years after you will often find that where you thought you have made the greatest blunders, you have accomplished the best results. The man who gets angriest at you, will often turn out in the end the man who is most grateful to you. Be patient and hope on. Never be discouraged.

Make a prayer list. Go alone with God. Write down at the top of a sheet of paper, "God helping me, I promise to pray daily and to work persistently for the conversion of the following persons." Then kneel down and ask God to show you who to put on that list. Do not make the list so long that your prayer and work become mechanical and superficial. After you have made the list keep your covenant, really pray for them every day. Watch for opportunities to speak to them—improve these opportunities. You may have to watch long for your opportunities with some of them, and you may have to speak often, but never give up. I prayed about fifteen years for one man, one of the most discouraging men I ever met, but I saw that man converted at last, and I saw him a preacher of the gospel, and many others were converted through his preaching, and now he is in the Glory.

Learn to use tracts. Get a few good tracts that are fitted to meet the needs of different kinds of people. Then hand these tracts out to the people whose needs they are adapted to meet. Follow your tracts up with prayer and with personal effort.

Go to your pastor and ask him if there is some work he would like to have you do for him in the church. Be a person that your pastor can depend upon. We live in a day in which there are many kinds of work going on outside the church, and many of these kinds of work are good and you should take part in them as you are able, but never forget that your first duty is to the church of which you are a member. Be a person that your pastor can count on. It may be that your pastor may not want to use you, but at least give him the chance of refusing you. If he does refuse you, don't be discouraged, but find work somewhere else. There is plenty to do and few to do it. It is as true to-day as it was in the days of our Saviour, "The harvest truly is plenteous but the labourers are few" (Matt. 9: 37), "Pray therefore the Lord of the harvest that He will send forth labourers into His harvest," and pray that He will send you (Matt. 9: 38). The right kind of men are needed in the ministry. The right kind of men and women are needed for foreign mission work, but you may not be the right kind of a man or woman for foreign missionary work, but none the less there is work for you to do just as important in its place as the work of the minister or the missionary is. See that you fill your place and fill it well.[4]

Reuben Archer Torrey

XI
FOREIGN MISSIONS

In order to have the largest success in the Christian life one must be interested in foreign missions. The last command of our Lord before leaving this earth was, "Go ye therefore, and make disciples of all the nations, baptizing them into the name of the Father, and of the Son and of the Holy Ghost: teaching them to observe all things whatsoever I have commanded you: and lo, I am with you alway even unto the end of the world" (Matt. 28: 19, 20, R. V.). Here is a command and a promise. It is one of the sweetest promises in the Bible. But the enjoyment of the promise is conditioned upon obedience to the command. Our Lord commands every one of His disciples to go and "make disciples" of all the nations. This command was not given to the apostles alone, but to every member of Christ's church in all ages. If we go, then Christ will be with us even unto the end of the age; but, if we do not go, we have no right to count upon His companionship. Are you going? There are three ways in which we can go, and in at least two of these ways we must go if we are to enjoy the wonderful privilege of the personal companionship of Jesus Christ every day unto the end of the age.

1. First, *many of us can go in our own persons*. Many of us ought to go. God does not call every one of us to go as foreign missionaries, but He does call many of us to go who are not

responding to the call. Every Christian should offer himself for the foreign field and leave the responsibility of choosing him or refusing him to the all-wise One, God Himself. No Christian has a right to stay at home until he has gone and offered himself definitely to God for the foreign field. If you have not done it before, do it to-day. Go alone with God and say, "Heavenly Father, here I am, Thy property, purchased by the precious blood of Christ. I belong to Thee. If Thou dost wish me in the foreign field, make it clear to me and I will go." Then keep watching for the leading of God. God's leading is clear leading. He is light and in Him is no darkness at all (1 John 1: 5). If you are really willing to be led, He will make it clear as day. Until He does make it clear as day, you need have no morbid anxiety that perhaps you are staying at home when you ought to go to the foreign field. If He wants you, He will make it clear as day in His own way and time. If He does make it clear, then prepare to go step by step as He leads you. And when His hour comes, go, no matter what it costs. If He does not make it clear that you ought to go in your own person, stay at home and do your duty at home and go in the other ways that will now be told.

2. *We all can go, and all ought to go to the foreign field by our gifts.* There are many who would like to go to the foreign field in their own person, but whom God providentially prevents, but who are still going in the missionaries they support or help to support. It is possible for you to preach the Gospel in the remotest corners of

the earth by supporting or helping to support a foreign missionary or a native worker in that place. Many who read this book are able financially to support a foreign missionary out of their own pocket. If you are able to do it, do it. If you are not able to support a foreign missionary, you may be able to support a native helper—do it. You may be able to support one missionary in Japan and another in China, and another in India and another in Africa and another somewhere else—do it. Oh! the joy of preaching the Gospel in lands that we shall never see with our own eyes. How few in the church of Christ to-day realize their privilege of preaching the Gospel and saving men and women and children in distant lands by sending substitute missionaries to them, that is, by sending some one that goes for you where you cannot go yourself. They could not go but for your gifts by which they are supported and you could not go but for them, by their going in your place. You may be able to give but very little to foreign missions, but every little counts. Many insignificant streams together make a mighty river. If you cannot be a river, at least be a stream.

Learn to give largely. The large giver is the happy Christian. "The liberal soul shall be made fat" (Prov. 11: 25). "He which soweth sparingly shall reap also sparingly, and he which soweth bountifully shall reap also bountifully," and "God is able to make all grace abound towards you, that ye, always having all sufficiency in all things may abound to every good work" (2 Cor. 9: 8, 9). Success and growth in the Christian life depend upon few things more than upon liberal giving. The stingy Christian cannot be a growing Christian. It is wonderful how a Christian man begins to grow when he begins to give. Power in prayer depends on liberality in giving. One of the most wonderful statements about prayer and its answers is 1 John 3: 22. John says there that, whatsoever he asked of God he received; and he tells us why, because he on his part, kept God's commandments and did those things which were pleasing in His sight, and the immediate context shows that the special commandments he was keeping were the commandments about giving. He tells us in the twenty-first verse that when our heart condemns us not in the matter of giving then have we confidence in our prayers to God. God's answers to our prayers come in through the same door that our gifts go out to others, and some of us open the door such a little ways by our small giving that God is not able to pass in to us any large answers to our prayers. One of the most remarkable promises in the Bible is that found in Phil. 4: 19, "My God shall supply (R. V., fulfill, that is fill full) all your need according to His riches in glory by Christ Jesus," but this promise was made to believers who had distinguished themselves above their fellows by the largeness and the frequency of their giving (Cf. vs. 14-18). Of course, we should not confine our giving to foreign missions. We should give to the work of the home church: we should give to rescue work in our large cities. We should do good to all men as we have opportunity, especially to those who are of the household of faith (Gal. 6: 10). But foreign missions should have a large part in our gifts.

Give systematically. Set aside for Christ a fixed proportion of all the money or goods you get. Be exact and honest about it. Don't use that part of your income for yourself under any circumstances. The Christian is not under law, and there is no law binding on the Christian that he should give a tenth of his income, but as a matter of free choice and glad gratitude a tenth is a good proportion to begin with. Don't let it be less than a tenth. God required that of the Jews and the Christian ought not to be more selfish than a Jew. After you have given your tenth, you will soon learn the joy of giving free will offerings in addition to the tenth.

3. But there is another way in which we can go to the foreign field, that is by our prayers. We can all go in this way. Any hour of the day or night you can reach any corner of the earth by your prayers. I go to Japan, to China and to Australia and to Tasmania and to New Zealand and to India and to Africa and to other parts of the earth every day, *by prayer*, and prayer really brings things to pass where you go. Do not make prayer an excuse for not going in your own person if God wishes you, and do not make prayer an excuse for small giving. There is no power in that kind of prayer. If you are ready to go yourself if God wishes you, and if you are actually going by your gifts as God gives you ability, then you can go effectually by your prayers also. The greatest need of the work of Jesus Christ to-day is prayer. The greatest need of foreign

missions to-day is prayer. Foreign missions are a success, but they are no such success as they ought to be and might be. They are no such success as they would be if Christians at home, as well as abroad, were living up to the full measure of their opportunity in prayer.

Be definite in your prayers for foreign missions. Pray first of all that God will send forth labourers into His harvest, the right sort of labourers. There are many men and women in the foreign field that ought never to have gone there. There was not enough prayer about it. More foreign missionaries are greatly needed, but only more of the right kind of missionaries. Pray to God daily and believingly to send forth labourers into the harvest.

Pray for the labourers who are already on the field. No class of men and women need our prayers more than foreign missionaries. No class of men and women are objects of more bitter hatred from Satan than they. Satan delights to attack the reputation and the character of the brave men and women who have gone to the front in the battle for Christ and the Truth. No persons are subjected to so numerous and to such subtle and awful temptations as foreign missionaries. We owe it to them to support them by our prayers. Do not merely pray for foreign missionaries in general. Have a few special missionaries of whose work you make a study that you may pray intelligently for them.

Pray for the native converts. We Christians at home think we have difficulties and trials and temptations and persecutions, but the burdens that we have to bear are nothing to what the converts in heathen lands have to bear. The obstacles oftentimes are enormous and discouragements crushing. Christ alone can make them stand, but He works in answer to the prayers of His people. Pray often, pray earnestly, pray intensely and pray believingly for native converts. How wonderfully God has answered prayer for native converts we are beginning to learn from missionary literature. It is well to be definite here again and to have some definite field about whose needs you keep yourself informed and pray for the converts of that field. Do not have so many that you become confused and mechanical. Pray for conversions in the foreign field. Pray for revivals in definite fields. The last few years have been years of special prayer for special revival in foreign fields and from every corner of the earth tidings have come of how amazingly God is answering these prayers. But the great things that God is beginning to do are small indeed in comparison with what He will do if there is more prayer.

Reuben Archer Torrey

XII

COMPANIONS

Our companions have a great deal to do with determining our character. The companionships that we form create an intellectual, moral and spiritual atmosphere that we are constantly breathing, and our spiritual health is helped or hindered by it. Every young Christian should have a few wisely chosen friends, intimate friends, with whom he can talk freely. Search out for yourself a few persons of about your own age with whom you can associate intimately. Be sure that they are spiritual persons in the best sense. Persons who love to study the Bible, persons who love to converse on spiritual themes, persons who know how to pray and do pray, persons who are really working to bring others to Christ.

Do not be at all uneasy about the fact that some Christian people are more agreeable to you than others. God has made us in that way. Some are attracted to some persons and some to others, and it proves nothing against the others and nothing against yourself that you are not attracted to some persons. Cultivate the friendship of those whose friendship you find helpful to your own spiritual life.

On the other hand avoid the companionships that you find spiritually and morally hurtful. Of course, we are not to withdraw ourselves utterly from unconverted people, or even of very bad people. We are to cultivate oftentimes the acquaintance of unspiritual people, and even of very bad people, in order that we may win them for Christ; but we must always be on our guard in such companionships to bear always in mind to seek to lift them up or else they will be sure to drag us down. If you find in spite of all your best effort that any companionship is doing harm to your own spiritual life, then give it up. Some people are surrounded with such an atmosphere of unbelief or cynicism or censoriousness or impurity or greed or some other evil thing that it is impossible to associate with them to any large extent without being contaminated. In such a case, the path of wisdom is plain; stop associating with them to any large extent. Stop associating with them at all except in so far as there is some prospect of helping them.

But there are other companionships that mould our lives besides the companionships of living persons. The books that we read are our companions. They exert a tremendous influence for good or for evil. There is nothing that will help us more than a good book, and there is nothing that will hurt us more than a bad book. Among the most helpful books are the biographies of good men. Read again and again the lives of such good and truly great men as Wesley and Finney and Moody. We live in a day in which good biographies abound. Read them. Well written histories are good companions. No study is more practical and instructive than the study of history, and it is not only instructive but spiritually helpful if we only watch to see the hand of God in history, to see the inevitable triumph of right and the inevitable punishment of wrong in individuals and in nations.

Some few books of fiction are helpful, but here one needs to be very much on his guard. A large portion of modern fiction is positively pernicious morally. Books of fiction that are not positively bad, at least give false views of life and unfit one for life as it really is. Much reading of fiction is mentally injurious. The inveterate novel reader ruins his powers of close and clear thinking. Fiction is so fascinating that it always tends to drive out other reading that is more helpful mentally and morally. We should be on our guard in even reading good literature, that the good does not crowd out the best; that is that the best of man's literature does not crowd out the very best of all—God's Book. God's Book, the Bible, must always have the first place.

Then there is another kind of companionship that has a tremendous influence over our lives, that is the companionship of pictures. The pictures that we see every day of our lives, and the pictures that we see only occasionally, have a great influence in the shaping of our lives. A mother had two dearly loved sons. It was her dream and ambition that these sons should enter the ministry, but both of them went to sea. She could not understand it until a friend one day called her attention to the picture of a magnificent ship in full sail careening through the ocean that hung above the mantel in the dining-room. Every day of their lives her boys had gazed upon that picture, had been thrilled by it, and an unconquerable love for the sea and longing for it had thus been created and this had determined their lives. How many a picture that is a masterpiece of art, but in which there is an evil suggestion, has sent some young men on the road to ruin. Many of our art collections are so polluted with improper pictures that it is not safe for a young man or a young woman to visit them. The evil thought that they suggest may be but for a moment, and yet Satan will know how to bring that picture back again and again and work injury by it. Don't look for a moment at any picture, no matter how praised by art critics, that taints your imagination with evil suggestion. Avoid as you would poison every painting, or engraving, every etching, every photograph that leaves a spot of impurity on your mind, but feast your soul upon the pictures that make you holier, kinder, more sympathetic and more tender.

XIII

AMUSEMENTS

Young people need recreation. Our Saviour does not frown upon wholesome recreation. He was interested in the games of the children when He was here upon earth. He watched the children at their play (Matt. 12: 16-19), and He watches the children at their play to-day, and delights in their play when it is wholesome and elevating. In the stress and strain of modern life older people too need recreation if they are to do their very best work. But there are recreations that are wholesome, and there are amusements that are pernicious. It is impossible to take up amusements one by one, and it is unnecessary. A few principles can be laid down.

1. *Do not indulge in any form of amusement about whose propriety you have any doubts.* Whenever you are in doubt, always give God the benefit of the doubt. There are plenty of recreations about which there can be no question. "He that doubteth is condemned: for whatsoever is not of faith is sin" (Rom. 14: 32, R.

amusement is wrong." Are you sure it is right? If not, leave it alone.

2. *Do not indulge in any amusement that you cannot engage in to the glory of God.* "Whether therefore ye eat or drink, or whatsoever ye do, do all to the glory of God" (1 Cor. 10: 31). Whenever you are in doubt as to whether you should engage in any

amusement ask yourself, Can I do this at this time to the glory of God?

3. *Do not engage in any amusement that will hurt your influence with anybody.* There are amusements, which perhaps are all right in themselves, but which we cannot engage in without losing our influence with some one. Now every true Christian wishes his life to tell with everybody to the utmost. There is so much to be done and so few to do it that every Christian desires every last ounce of power for good that he can have with everybody, and, if any amusement will injure your influence for good with any one, the price is too great. Do not engage in it. A Christian young lady had a great desire to lead others to Christ. She made up her mind that she would speak to a young friend of hers about coming to Christ, and while resting between the figures of a dance she said to the young man who was her companion in the dance, "George, are you a Christian?" "No," he said, "I am not, are you?" "Yes," she replied, "I am." "Then," he said, "what are you doing here?" Whether justly or unjustly the world discounts the professions of those Christians who indulge in certain forms of the world's own amusements. We cannot afford to have our professions thus discounted.

4. *Do not engage in any amusement that you cannot make a matter of prayer*, that you cannot ask God's blessing upon. Pray before your play just as much as you would pray before your work.

5. *Do not go to any place of amusement where you cannot take Christ with you, and where you do not think Christ would feel at home.* Christ went to places of mirth when He was here upon earth. He went to the marriage feast in Cana (John 2), and contributed to the joy of the occasion, but there are many modern places of amusement where Christ would not be at home. Would the atmosphere of the modern stage be congenial to that holy One whom we call "Lord"? If it would not, don't you go.

6. *Don't engage in any amusement that you would not like to be found enjoying if the Lord should come.* He may come at any moment. Blessed is that one whom when He cometh, He shall find watching and ready, and glad to open to Him immediately (Luke 12: 36, 40). I have a friend who was one day walking down the street thinking upon the return of his Lord. As he thought he was smoking a cigar. The thought came to him, "Would you like to meet Christ now with that cigar in your mouth?" He answered honestly, "No, I would not." He threw that cigar away and never lighted another.

7. *Do not engage in any amusement, no matter how harmless it would be for yourself, that might harm some one else.* Take for example card playing. It is probable that thousands have played cards moderately all their lives and never suffered any direct moral injury from it, but every one who has studied the matter knows that cards are the gamblers' chosen tools. He also knows that most, if not all, gamblers took their first lessons in card playing at the quiet

family card table. He knows that if a young man goes out into the world knowing how to play cards and indulging at all in this amusement that before long he is going to be put into a place where he is going to be asked to play cards for money, and if he does not consent he will get into serious trouble. Card playing is a dangerous amusement for the average young man. It is pretty sure to lead to gambling on a larger or a smaller scale, and one of the most crying social evils of our time is the evil of gambling. Some young man may be encouraged to play cards by your playing who will afterwards become a gambler and part of the responsibility will lie at your door. If I could repeat all the stories that have come to me from broken-hearted men whose lives have been shipwrecked at the gaming table; if I could tell of all the broken-hearted mothers who have come to me, some of them in high position, whose sons have committed suicide at Monte Carlo and other places, ruined by the cards, I think that all thoughtful and true Christians would give them up forever.

For most of us the recreations that are most helpful are those that demand a considerable outlay of physical energy. Recreations that take us into the open air, recreations that leave us refreshed in body and invigorated in mind. Physical exercises of the strenuous kind, but not over-exercise, is one of the great safeguards of the moral conduct of boys and young men. There is very little recreation in watching others play the most vigorous game of football but there is real health for the body and for the soul in a due amount of physical exercise for yourself.

Reuben Archer Torrey

XIV

PERSECUTION

One of the discouragements that meets every true Christian before he has gone very far in the Christian life is persecution. God tells us in His Word that "All that will live godly in Christ Jesus shall suffer persecution" (2 Tim. 3: 12). Sooner or later every one who surrenders absolutely to God and seeks to follow Jesus Christ in everything will find that this verse is true. We live in a God-hating world and in a compromising age. The world's hatred of God in our day is veiled. It does not express itself in our land in the same way that it expressed itself in Palestine in the days of Jesus Christ, but the world hates God to-day as much as it ever did, and it hates the one who is loyal to Christ. It may not imprison him or kill him but in some way it will persecute him. Persecution is inevitable for a loyal follower of Jesus Christ. Many a young Christian when he meets with persecution is surprised and discouraged and not a few fall away. Many a one seems to run well for a time and are like those of whom Jesus spoke, "They have no root in themselves, but endure for a while; then when tribulation or persecution ariseth because of the Word straightway they stumble" (Mark 4: 17). I have seen many an apparently promising Christian life brought to an end in this way. But if persecution is rightly received, it is no longer a hindrance to the Christian life but a help to it.

Do not be discouraged when you are persecuted. No matter how fierce and hard the persecution may be, be thankful for it. Jesus says, "Blessed are they which are persecuted for righteousness' sake: for theirs is the kingdom of heaven. Blessed are ye, when men shall revile you, and persecute you, and shall say all manner of evil against you falsely, for My sake. Rejoice, and be exceeding glad: for great is your reward in heaven: for so persecuted they the prophets which were before you" (Matt. 5: 10-12). It is a great privilege to be persecuted for Christ and for the truth. Peter found this out and wrote to the Christians of his day: "Beloved, think it not strange concerning the fiery trial which is to try you, as though some strange thing happened unto you. But rejoice, inasmuch, as ye are partakers of Christ's suffering; that, when His glory shall be revealed, ye may be glad also with exceeding joy. If ye be reproached for the name of Christ, happy are ye; for the spirit of glory and of God resteth upon you: on their part He is evil spoken of, but on your part He is glorified" (1 Peter 4: 12-14). Be very sure that the persecution is really for Christ's sake and not because of some eccentricity of your own, or because of your stubbornness. There are many who bring upon themselves the displeasure of others because they are stubborn and cranky and then flatter themselves that they are being persecuted for Christ's sake and for righteousness' sake. Be considerate of the opinions of others and be considerate of the conduct of others. Be sure that you do not push your opinions upon others in an unwarrantable way, or make your conscience a rule of life for other people. But never yield a jot of principle. Stand for what you believe to be the truth. Do it in love, but do it at any cost. And if when you are standing for conviction and principle you are disliked for it and slandered for it and treated with all manner of unkindness because of it, do not be sad but rejoice. Do not speak evil of those who speak evil of you, "because Christ also suffered for us, leaving us an example, that ye should follow His steps: who, when He was reviled, reviled not again, when He suffered, He threatened not; but committed Himself to Him that judgeth righteously" (1 Peter 2: 21, 23).

At this point many a Christian makes a mistake. He stands loyally for the truth, but he receives the persecution that comes for the truth with harshness, he grows bitter, he gets to condemning every one but himself. There is no blessing in bearing persecution in that way. Persecution should be borne meekly, lovingly, serenely. Don't talk about your own persecutions. Rejoice in them. Thank God for them, and go on obeying God. And don't forget to pray for them who persecute you (Matt. 5: 44).

If at any time the persecution seems harder than you can bear, remember how abundant the reward is, "If we suffer, we shall also reign with Him. If we deny Him, He also will deny us" (2 Tim. 2: 12). Every one must enter into the kingdom of God through much tribulation (Acts 14: 22), but do not go back on that account. Remember always however fiercely the fire of persecution may burn, "That the sufferings of this present time are not worthy to be compared with the glory which shall be revealed in us" (Rom. 8: 18). Remember too that your light affliction is but for the moment, and that it worketh out for you "a far more exceeding and eternal weight of glory" (2 Cor. 4: 17). Keep looking, not at the things which are seen, but at the things which are not seen, for the things which are seen are but for a time, but the things which are not seen are for eternity (2 Cor. 4: 18). When the apostles were persecuted, even unto imprisonment and stripes, they departed from the presence of the council that had ordered their terrible punishment, rejoicing that they were counted worthy to suffer shame for the name of Jesus, and they continued daily in the temple and every house teaching and preaching Jesus Christ (Acts 5: 40-42).

The time may come when you think that you are being persecuted more than others, but you do not know what others may have to endure. Even if it were true,—that you were being persecuted more than any one else, you ought not to complain but to humbly thank God that He has bestowed upon you such an honour. Keep your eyes fixed upon "Jesus, the Author and Finisher of our faith; who for the joy that was set before Him endured the cross, despising the shame, and is set down at the right hand of the throne of God. For consider Him that endured such contradiction of sinners against Himself, lest ye be wearied and faint in your mind" (Heb. 12: 2, 3). I was once talking with an old coloured man who in the slave days had found his Saviour. The cruel master had him flogged again and again for his loyalty to Christ but he said to me, "I simply thought of my Saviour dying on the cross in my place, and I rejoiced to suffer persecution for Him."

Reuben Archer Torrey

XV
GUIDANCE

I have met a great many who are trying to lead a Christian life who are much troubled over the question of guidance. They wish to do the will of God in all things, but what puzzles them is to tell what the will of God may be in every case. When any one starts out with the determination to obey God in everything and to be led by the Holy Spirit, Satan seeks to trouble him by perplexing him as to what the will of God is. Satan comes and suggests that something is the will of God that is probably not the will of God at all, and then when he does not do it, Satan says, "There you disobeyed God." In this way, many a conscientious young Christian gets into a very morbid and unhappy state of mind, fearing that he has disobeyed God and has lost His favour. This is one of the most frequent devices of the devil to keep Christians from being cheerful.

How may we know the will of God?

First of all let me say that we are not governed by a whole lot of rules about what one shall eat, and what one shall drink, and what one shall do, and what one shall not do. A life governed by a lot of rules is a life of bondage. One is sure sooner or later to break some of these man-made rules and to get into condemnation. Paul tells us in Rom. 8: 15, "Ye have not received the spirit of bondage again to fear; but ye have received the spirit of adoption (placing us a son), whereby we cry, Abba, Father." The true Christian life is the life of a trusting, glad, fear-free child; not led by rules, but led by the personal guidance of the Holy Spirit who dwells within us. "As many as are led by the Spirit of God these are sons of God" (Rom. 8: 14, R. V.). If you have received the Holy Spirit, He dwells within you and is ready to lead you at every turn of life. A life governed by a multitude of rules is a life of bondage and anxiety. A life surrendered to the control of the Holy Spirit is a life of joy and peace and freedom. There is no anxiety in such a life, there is no fear in the presence of God. We trust God and rejoice in His presence just as a true child trusts his earthly father and rejoices in his presence. If we make a mistake at any point, even if we disobey God, we go and tell Him all about it as trustfully as a child and know that He forgives us and that we are restored at once to His full favour (1 John 1: 9).

But how can we tell the Holy Spirit's guidance that we may obey Him and thus have God's favour at every turn of life? This question is answered in James 1: 5-7, R. V., "But if any of you lacketh wisdom, let him ask of God, who giveth to all liberally and upbraideth not; and it shall be given him, but let him ask in faith, nothing doubting: for he that doubteth is like the surge of the sea driven by the wind and tossed. For let not that man think that he shall receive anything of the Lord." This is very simple. It includes five points.

(1) That you recognize your own ignorance and your own inability to guide your own life—that you lack wisdom.

(2) The surrender of your will to God, and a real desire to be led by Him.

(3) Definite prayer to Him for guidance.

(4) Confident expectation that God will guide you. You "ask in faith, nothing doubting."

(5) That you follow step by step as He guides. God may only show you a step at a time. That is enough. All you need to know is the next step. It is here that many make a mistake. They wish God to show them the whole way before they take the first step. A university student once came to me over the question of guidance. He said, "I cannot find out the will of God. I have been praying but God does not show me His will." This was in the month of July. I said, "About what is it that you are seeking to know the will of God?" "About what I should do next summer." I said, "Do you know what you ought to do to-morrow?" "Yes." "Do you not know what you ought to do next autumn?" "Yes, finish my course. But what I want to know is what I ought to do when my university course is over." He was soon led to see that all he needed to know for the present was what God had already shown him. That when he did that, God would show him the next step. Do not worry about what you ought to do next week. Do what God shows you you ought to do to-day. Next week will take care of itself. Indeed,

to-morrow will take care of itself. Obey the Spirit of God for to-day. "Be not therefore anxious for the morrow; for the morrow will be anxious for the things of itself. Sufficient unto the day is the evil thereof" (Matt. 6: 34, R. V.). It is enough to live a day at a time, if we do our very best for that day.

God's guidance is clear guidance, "God is light and in Him is no darkness at all" (1 John 1: 5). Do not be anxious over obscure leadings. Do not let your soul be ruffled by the thought, "Perhaps this obscure leading is what God wants me to do." Obscure leadings are not divine leadings. God's path is as clear as day. Satan's path is full of obscurity and uncertainty and anxiety and questioning. If there comes some leading of which you are not quite sure whether it is the will of God or not, simply go to your Heavenly Father and say, "Heavenly Father, I desire to know Thy will. I will do Thy will if Thou wilt make it clear. But Thou art light and in Thee is no darkness at all. If this is Thy will make it clear as day and I will do it." Then wait quietly upon God and do not act until God makes it clear, but the moment it is made clear, act at once.

The whole secret of guidance is an absolutely surrendered will, a will that is given up to God and ready to obey Him at any cost. Many of our uncertainties about God's guidance are simply because we are not really willing to do what God is really guiding us to do. We are tempted to say, "I cannot find out what God's will is," when the real trouble is we have found out His will and it is something we do not wish to do and we are trying to make ourselves think that God wants us to do something else.

All supposed leadings of God should be tested by the Word of God. The Bible is God's revealed will. Any leading that contradicts the plain teaching of the Bible is certainly not the leading of the Holy Spirit. The Holy Spirit does not contradict Himself. A man once came to me and said that God was leading him to marry a certain woman. He said that she was a very devoted Christian woman and they had been greatly drawn towards one another and they felt that God was leading them to be married. But I said to the man, "You already have a wife." "Yes," he said, "but we have never lived happily and we have not lived together for years." "But," I replied, "that does not alter the case. God in His Word has told us distinctly the duty of the husband to the wife and how wrong it is in His sight for a husband to divorce his wife and marry another." "Yes," said the man, "but the Holy Spirit is leading us to one another." I indignantly replied that "Whatever spirit is leading you to marry one another, it is certainly not the Holy Spirit but the spirit of the evil one. The Holy Spirit never leads any one to disobey the Word of God."

In seeking to know the guidance of the Spirit always search the Scriptures, study them prayerfully. Do not make a book of magic out of the Bible. Do not ask God to show you His will and then open your Bible at random and put your finger upon some text and take it out of its connection without any relation to its real meaning and decide the will of God in that way. This is an irreverent and improper use of Scripture. You may open your Bible at just the right place to find right guidance, but if you do, it will not be by some fanciful interpretation of the passage you find. It will be by taking the passage in its context and interpreting it to mean just what it says as seen in its context. All sorts of mischief has arisen from using the Bible in this perverse way. I knew an earnest Christian woman once who was somewhat concerned about the predictions made by a false prophetess that Chicago was to be destroyed on a certain day. She opened her Bible at random. It opened to the twelfth chapter of Ezekiel, "Son of man, eat thy bread with quaking, and drink thy water with trembling and with carefulness.... And the cities that are inhabited shall be laid waste, and the land shall be desolate" (Ezek. 12: 18, 20). Now this seemed to exactly fit the case and the woman was considerably impressed, but if the verses had been studied in their connection, it would have been evident at once that God was not speaking about Chicago and that they were not applicable to Chicago. It was not an intelligent study of the Word of God and therefore led to a false conclusion.

To sum up, lead a life not led by rules but by the personal guidance of the Holy Spirit. Surrender your will absolutely to God. Whenever you are in doubt as to His guidance, go to Him and ask Him to show you His will, expect Him to do it, follow step by step as He leads. Test all the leadings by the plain and simple teachings of the Bible. Live free from anxiety and worry lest in some unguarded moment you have not done the right thing.

After you have done what you think God led you to do, do not be always going back and wondering whether you did the right thing. You will get into a morbid state if you do. If you really wished to do God's will and sought His guidance, and did what you thought He guided you to do, you may rest assured you did the right thing, no matter what the outcome has been. Satan is bound that we shall not be happy, cheerful Christians if he can prevent it, but God wishes us to be happy, cheerful, bright Christians every day and every hour. He does not wish us to brood but to rejoice (Phil. 4: 4). A most excellent Christian man came to me one Monday morning in great gloom over the failures of the work of the preceding day. He said to me, "I made wretched work of teaching my Sunday-school class yesterday." I said, "Did you honestly seek wisdom from God before you went to your class?" He said, "I did." I said, "Did you expect to receive it?" He said, "I did." "Then," I said, "in the face of God's promise what right have you to doubt that God did give you wisdom?" (James 1: 5-7). His gloom disappeared and he looked up with a smile and said, "I had no right to doubt." Let us learn to trust God. Let us remember that if our wills are surrendered to Him He is ever more willing to guide us than we are to be guided. Let us trust that He does guide us at every step and even though what we do does not turn out as we expected, let us never brood over it but trust God. Let us walk in the light of simple trust in God. In this way we shall be glad and peaceful and strong and useful at every turn of life.

FOOTNOTES

[1] The author has given some of the proofs that the Bible is the Word of God in his book, "Talks to Men."

[2] If any reader desires more full and definite instruction on the subject of prayer he is referred to the author's book, "How to Pray."

[3] The author has written a little book on this line named "How to Bring Men to Christ" that has proved helpful to many.

[4] The author's book, "How to Work for Christ," is a large work describing at length many ways of working for our Master.

www.ingramcontent.com/pod-product-compliance
Lightning Source LLC
Chambersburg PA
CBHW020911080526
44589CB00011B/549